THE HISTORY &
DEVELOPMENT OF THE
SOMALI SCRIPT

THE HISTORY & DEVELOPMENT OF THE
SOMALI SCRIPT

Revised & Expanded B.A. Degree at Lafoole College, Somali University 1988.

Suleiman Geddi Qayad

Looh Press | 2021

LOOH PRESS LTD.
Copyright © Suleiman Geddi Qayad 2021.
First Edition, October 2021.

All rights reserved. No part of this publication may be reproduced, stored in any retrieval system, or transmitted in any form or by any means, including photocopying, recording, or other electronic or mechanical methods, without the prior written permission of the publisher, except in the case of brief quotations embodied in critical reviews and certain other noncommercial uses permitted by copyright law. For permission and requests, write to the publisher, at the address below.

Printed & Distributed by
Looh Press
56 Lethbridge Close
Leicester, LE1 2EB,
England, UK
www.LoohPress.com
admin@LoohPress.com

Printed & bounded by: TJ Books. Cornwall, England.
Waxaa Daabacay:

ISBN: 978-1-912411-38-2

CONTENT

PUBLISHERS NOTE	vii
INTRODUCTION	ix
ACKNOWLEDGMENTS	xi
THESIS INTRODUCTION	1
WADAADS' CONTRIBUTION TO THE SOMALI WRITING	9
YOUNG SOMALI NATIONALISTS AND THEIR CONTRIBUTION TO THE SOMALI WRITING.	13
QADI SOMALI SCRIPT.	16
LATIN ALPHABET ADAPTATION ON SOMALI LANGUAGE	19
Final steps towards Somali writing from 1960 until 1972.	21
CONCLUSION	24
APPENDICES	26
BIBLIOGRAPHY	143

CONTENT

PUBLISHER'S NOTE	vii
INTRODUCTION	ix
ACKNOWLEDGMENTS	xi
THESIS INTRODUCTION	1
MADAR'S CONTRIBUTION TO THE SOMALI WRITING	4
YOUNG SOMALI NATIONALISTS AND THEIR CONTRIBUTION TO THE SOMALI WRITING	12
O.D.M SOMALI SCRIPTS	16
LATIN ALPHABET ADAPTATION ON SOMALI LANGUAGE	19
Final steps towards Somali writing from 1960 until 1972.	21
CONCLUSION	24
APPENDICES	26
BIBLIOGRAPHY	63

PUBLISHERS NOTE

"*Looh Press Theses Series*" is aimed to bring to our readers some of the rare and unpublished theses out there in Somali, Arabic, and English. Some of these theses are unique, others are impactful but never published. For the purpose of accessibility to specialists and non-specialists, some of these theses are published as they are, with minor editorial efforts, others are completely rewritten, with introduction. Some are abridged for the purpose of wider readership.

As such the series is aimed to enrich the library of Somali studies and provide a valuable resource for specialists and non-specialists alike. The Lafoole College Theses are an exceptional historical archive that survived the Somali civil war, giving us a glimpse of Mogadishu national library.

This paper is a rare academic endeavour, thin as it is, yet very much expancing in its scope of data and research. Author interviewed some of the most important and leading figures involved in the development of the Somali script. However one has to be aware that this paper is just a BA degree paper and not a doctoral thesis.

We have supplemented it with a report published for the purpose of Somali script recommendation. As such, we have chosen to reproduce this crucial report and slightly standardised it for the purpose of comfortable modern reading. The report was published 15th May 1962 and is part of Public Domain. It was published by the Somali Language Committee and was written by A. Sh. A. Qutbi. Sixty years on this report stands unique in its detailed assessment of available Somali script at the time and the committee members involved in recommending unifying script to the Somali civil government at the time which was just two years in office at the time, coming out of colonial rule. Unfortunately it would take Somalia another decade to officiate script based on new committee and finding.

Suleiman Geddi paper therefore is very crucial for us as it provides a brief assessment of civil and government effort in developing ingenious yet practical script for all Somali speakers.

Mohammed Artan
Manager of Looh Press
October, 2021

INTRODUCTION

After long discussion in deciding which script is to be adopted for the Somali language, It took its final turn in 1972 when the Somali orthography was written and became the official language for Somalia. After the collapse of the Somali central government in 1991 it negatively affected every aspect of Somali people's social, educational, political and economical development. In the last two decades many academic papers were written and a number of researches were conducted touching various topics of Somali orthography.

This book will contribute to recreating the lost efforts and history of Somali script due to civil war, and will shed light on the history of the Somali orthography development upto its final shape. I am sure the university students, academics and general public alike will find it useful and will enrich their knowledge on this crucial period for Somali literary history. This book which was at first produced as a thesis shows that the Somali University students, especially those attending at Lafoole College of Education were keen to unearth the Somali knowledge and produce theses in different topics. Large section of Lafoole's library was specially created to be stored in these theses and hopefully it is not all lost in the civil war which ravaged the country. These theses had the potential to be used as the backbone of further research in various social, scientific and cultural topics.

Suleyman Geddi
Leicester, UK 2021

ACKNOWLEDGMENTS

I would like to express my appreciation and gratitude to Dr. Mohamed Noh Ali, my advisor, for his unlimited continuous advice and valuable guidance that made possible the production of this thesis. My thanks are also due to Shaykh Abdirahman Sh. Nuur who allowed me to do an interview with him during writing this thesis, and Hussein Sh. Ahmed Kaddareh.

Thanks also to Haji Hassan Aw Cali, Hanna Haji Hassan Aw Cali, Mohamed Ahmed Cusmaan (Keyse) and Ismail Osman Hussein for their help.

THESIS INTRODUCTION

Introduction.

In this thesis I will attempt to investigate the history of the development of Somali script writing with special emphasis on Qadi Somali Script.

In the early times pre literate people could communicate with one another only by speaking or making gestures. They had no way to keep records of important events unless they memorized the story of a great battle or important events. They had no way to send messages over long distances unless they passed them from one person to the next by word of mouth or had one man memorize the message and then deliver it.

The first stages of writing came when man learned to draw pictures in order to express their ideas. 3000 B.C. Egyptians used a system of several hundred signs that stood for full words or for syllables. Most of the Latin Alphabets that exist today are derived from it.

Somali intellectuals took a great step forward on the long road of their history when they first began to use written symbols to represent their language. Religious leaders were the pioneers of Somali Script writing and they applied Arabic alphabets to the Somali language. Attempts continued until it took its final shape in 1972.

Although scholars in the field of Somali History wrote and did some research on this topic, their contribution was limited to a general overview and no scholar was able to investigate profoundly one of the Somali scripts except (I.M. Lewis) who wrote an article about the Qadi script accompanied with six texts written by Shaykh Adbirahman himself. So, it opened a new avenue to give emphasis on one of the Somali Invented Scripts.

This thesis suffers from a number of factors among them lack of funds, adequate time and enough resources, but keen efforts will be put in it to approach the reality at least.

Somali Geography.

The horn of Africa is a semi-desert region almost, except the arable area between the two rivers; Juba and Shabelle and small plateau area in the north west and Awdal regions while Bay region is the most fertile in the area. The percent of the rainfall annually is very low. The climate is hot and dry most of the year.

The latest statistics estimated the Somali society around eight million and half. Whether the Somalis live in the Somali Democratic Republic or out of it, they are from one origin, they share the same characteristics and they are the same ethnic group.

Historical Background of The Somali Society.

Since there are no documentary resources dealing with the original place of Somali society, the question will be unclear until there is effective research on the problem. It is necessary to do archaeological excavations or to trace back the origin of Somali society through linguistic evidence. These two methods are the best way to approach the place of origin for Somali society.

Somali Academy of Science and Art (Somac) is taking the first steps to build up Somali history through archaeological evidence and still the excavations continue in Banadir area, Somali Historians and archaeologists' belief that there are also places rich in artifacts and ecofacts scattered in the horn. Very reliable research may be carried out later on.

I.M. Lewis reinforces the arguments of Somalis' claim on Arab ancestors. The claim of Arab origin is a Somali blindly claim, and there is no evidence verifying this argument rather than oral tradition

Other Scholars much more contemporary have a different view of Somali history such as Fleming 1964, S.H. Lewis 1965, Ehert 1974, Noh 1985. They claimed that the Somali society expanded to the north and east from the area of Omo and Tana rivers or in-between Lake Turkana and the Indian Ocean. Linguistic evidence supports this claim because all Omo-Tana languages except Somali III Language are found and spoken between Lake Abaya and Lake Turkana. This view is the dominant and it is the rational view in recent years.

Most of the scholars who are doing historical research on Somali history in various degrees seek support for this view.

Early Somali Migration.

Early Somali community set out from somewhere in the Rift Valley and they reached the plains of north Kenya roughly 2000 years ago. They traveled and began to spread southwards, reaching and streaming to the Tana river down to its mouth at the Indian Ocean. The territory gradually became Somali speaking settlements; there is no evidence of pre-Somali habitation in this area.

Rendille is one of the Somali societies that remained in the area while Somali III on the other hand continued with their migration in the same way as earlier. Once a new territory was occupied some of the population would settle down whereas another part moved on looking for new grazing areas. Thus the territory of the Somali speaking community was gradually extended Upon reaching the Indian Ocean this eastern expansion followed northern expansion until they occupied what is today the Republic of Somalia (see the map on page 6). This population spread ultimately caused the occupation of the east African horn.

The Somali Coastal communities developed as a result of trade between them and south-west Asians. Due to this interaction a new Islamic culture and society appeared, this culture was urban in out-look, the Port

Zaila was erected 200 years after this Somali and south West Asians contact.

MAP SHOWING THE LIMIT TERRITORY INHABITED BY SOMALIS TODAY.

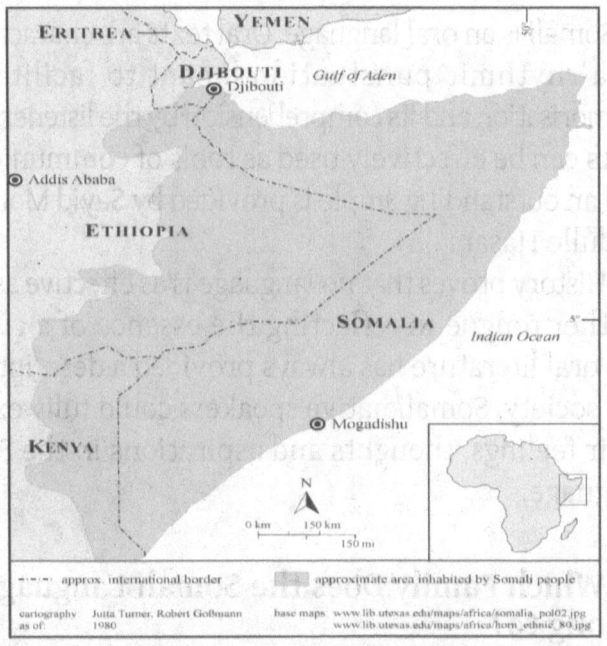

Other towns appeared along the Somali coast later on, among them Mogadishu, Marka, Brava and Berbera. This period was the second phase of Somali society migration which started roughly 1000 years ago.

By the 12th century the whole of the northern coastal towns had been Islamized. Hereafter the Islamic teachings expanded deep inland and Islamic cities built up in the western of the horn among them Harar and other towns ruined for unknown reasons. After the period mentioned above the Somali settlements were as they are today.

Somali Language.

Somali is an oral language. Oral texts are characterized by a rhythmic punctuation meant to facilitate its memorisation and its comprehension by the listeners, such texts can be effectively used as tools of communication and an outstanding ample is provided by Sayid Mohamed Abdulle Hasan.

History proves that no language is as effective as one's mother tongue in reflecting the essence of a culture, our oral literature has always provided a description of our society. Somali native speakers could fully express their feelings, thoughts and aspirations in the Somali language.

To Which Family Does the Somali Language Belong to?

The Somali Language is very old and rich. Somali language belongs to the Afroasiatic Family within this Family somali is a member of the cushitic sub-family whose original homeland must be sought on the central of the Rift valley. Like Afar, Soha or Oromo, Somali is derived from the eastern group called Omo-Tana which is spoken between Omo and Tana rivers. The most Somali closely related languages are Arbore and

Elomo in which core speakers of these languages have remained in the pro Omo homeland.

Somali Dialects.

It has been claimed recently (Ehert, Noh 1985) that there are about six major dialects in the Somali language family, among the most numerous in terms of its speakers are two dialects, Maay and Maxaad tiri? What and what did you say? respectively, each one of these dialects has sub-dialects but still there is no investigation being done on their vocabulary.

Somali phonology.

Somalis and Somalist Scholars conducted research on the phonology of the Somali Language who viewed the subject from different facets, some of these researches are reliable others were insignificant.

In 1960 Somali highly educated figures in the field of linguistics agreed that there are at least 44 different phonemes in the Somali language which can be grouped as follows:
Consonants 24 sounds.
Short Vowels 10 sounds.
Long Vowels 10 sounds.
This rules for the phonetic sounds of the Somali language became apparent after long discussion and study on Maay and Maxaad tiri- What? and what did you say? respectively.

Later on, a commission appointed to study the Somali language suggested that the phonetic sounds of the Somali language are 32 sounds.

Consonant   22 sounds (including glottal stop).
Short Vowel   5 sounds.
Long Vowel   5 sounds.

But the phonetic sounds in the Somali language may be much more than those stated above, the phonetic sounds used in the Somali language are the basic symbols for Somali writing now. And still the question about Somali phonology is not yet studied keenly in a formal and scientific way.

WADAADS' CONTRIBUTION TO THE SOMALI WRITING

Islamic Religion is a faith based on believing in one God (Allah) and his apostle Mohamed (Peace be upon him). It has two sources from which its divine and religious law comes up; The Holy Qur'an, the direct words from our lord that came to us through his messenger. The second source is prophetic traditions in which the prophet described the Islamic religion in its broadest sense.

Muslims are obliged to obey these two sources from which they will be on true guidance and it is these who will prosper. Many verses in the holy Qur'an encouraged knowledge seeking, and the prophet, Mohamed also preached to his followers to seek knowledge and travel for the sake of it even to china (the farthest place known for that time). Due to this encouragement Muslim empire was the shinning centres of knowledge for many years, whose science had once illumined the world.

Formal European system of education has been established recently in Somalia. Before, there were Qur'anic schools 'Malcaamad' Shaykhs were the teachers, the only educated people, the thinkers and elites that we had.

In the 13th century Shaykhs tried to apply Arabic characters to the Somali language; they cultivated the seeds of Somali writing. This chapter will shed light on and discuss the role that wadaads played in Somali Orthography.

Sh. Yusuf bin Ahmed Al-Kowneyn who came to Somali in the 13th century was the first person who tried to translate Arabic vowels into Somali language. In teaching the Quran for Somali youth Sh. Yusuf keenly studied Somali phonology and compared it with Arabic phonology. Finally Sh. Yusuf established a Somali system of Arabic reading named 'Alif waxma leh', in which the Somali people benefited from it. They learnt the Quran easily without much difficulty and that period was a turning point for Somali deep islamization. Shortly after this time Somali writing flourished in which Arabic characters represented Somali sounds. This system is called 'Wadaads Writing'.

As we mentioned before, the Somali language has at least 32 phonemes (including glottal stop). These sounds are 22 consonant sounds and 10 vowel sounds; 5 short and 5 long. Compared with the Arabic phonemes, Arabic consonant sounds are 28 sounds, 8 Arabic consonant sounds are excluded from Somali consonant sounds, while 'G' and 'DH' Somali consonant sounds doesn't included in Arabic. Somali is rich in vowels compared to Arabic vowels.

The initial stages of undertaking two Somali consonant sounds 'G' and 'DH' required to be transcribed into Arabic. Although there were no standard symbols agreed upon in Wadaad's writing, 'DH' was mostly written 'ڎ'[1] or (ط) and sometimes 'ظ' and 'G' was written 'ج'. Arabic lacks the Somali vowel sounds e, ee and o, oo. Also, wadaad writing mostly omitted the short vowels, and it was difficult to read and understand unless one acquired the meaning through the context, so further consideration was needed.

The reason being encouraged the famous Qadiriya Saint the founder of Uwaysiyya branch which is widely extended in southern somalia Shaykh Uways Ibn Muhamed al-Barawi who was assassinated at Biyoley in Bakool region in 1919 to transcribe sub-classical somali dialects in Arabic alphabet was the Arabic symbols adopted by Swahili - Speaking Aramani of Brava. He took steps forward in developing Arabic characters to represent the Somali Language. The Sound 'DH' is written 'ظ' and 'G' is written 'ݣ' as in Persian. The Somali vowels 'e' and 'O' were written (أي) and (أو) respectively.

In the 1930s Sheekh Maxamed Abdi Makahil following the steps of his predecessor in the British protectorate, benefiting from the previous failures, gave efforts to develop Arabic representation for the Somali language. He wrote the two Somali distinct consonants 'G' and 'DH' as previously written. In his book "The institution of Modern Correspondence in Somali language" illustrated Somali sentences, letters and proverbs written in Arabic

---

1 For further reading on this, please refer to the attached report The Report of the Somali Language Committee 1961......, section Appendix 01, p 137.

characters. Shaykh Mohamed failed to transcribe the vowel sounds 'e' and 'o' into Arabic, as Arabic letters lacked these vowels.

Recently Muuse X. Ismaaciil Galaal the Somali scholar following the previous Shaykhs' attempts took fundamental changes not any one before him thought. His work was the most appropriate Arabic characters devised for Somali. After 1954 Muse X. Ismaaciil Galaal changed his mind and sided with the scholars who claimed Latin representation.

YOUNG SOMALI NATIONALISTS AND THEIR CONTRIBUTION TO THE SOMALI WRITING.

Islam preaches unity and brotherhood among muslims and considers that all the believers are brothers without being segregated the poor from the wealthy, the black from the white the president from the society. Islam in Somalia has long been associated with the brotherhoods through tariqas which created in the long run feeling of patriotism among the Somalis.

The Somali hero Sayid Mohamed Abdulle Hassan who belonged to the salihiya branch of the Ahmadiyya Order, founded at Mecca by Sayyid Muhamed Salih, Started a remarkable struggle to free his country from the foreign domination, just after his return from Saudi Arabia. He realized that mission schools are possible to lead somalis and their children away from Islam, but many turned to him deaf ears. Later on he built a masque which was Salihiya prorogation centre.

For many years Sayyid Muhamed Abdulle Hassan was fighting against the British with a style of guerrilla warfare. British soldiers and Dervishes were confronted with many places. Sometimes Dervishes were slaughtering the British camel corps and other times the British were obtaining the upper-hand.

Finally, British planes' attack on Sayyid's fort at Taleh with killing many people ended Sayyid's struggle. Shortly after his escape from the Taleh bombing died when he became ill with malaria Dec. 21 1921.

During the years of his struggle, Somali nationalism grew stronger within the society. Sayyid Mohamed laid the bases of Somali nationalism which ultimately freed the country in 1960.

It has been recognized that the young somali nationalists in the twentieth century foiling to have a national indigenous script will go directly to Sayyid's campaign to free his country from the foreign invaders, because it gave an autonomy, feeling their identity preservation of somali religion and culture from colonial European culture. So, they thought of devising a unique Script belonging to them.

Osman Yusuf Kanadiid the brother of Ali Yusuf Kanadiid Sultan of Obbio invented in 1920 a script different in character from the Arabic and the Latin. This newly invented script has 22 consonant symbols (Hamza is included) and 5 long vowels and 5 short vowels. There were also ten numerals. Phonetically, the Osmania script was highly accurate. It has been claimed that there is no Ethiopian influence but by looking at it seems to be there is some affinity especially the following symbols:-

ሣ ʦ ʎ ʎ ʔ ℓ ቻ ሁ ℋ ቢ
b d g x r sh c f q l

ʎ ʕ ʎ ሀ
w aa uu ee

Another Orthography which is independent and different from Osmania was invented by Sh. Abdirahman Sh. Nuur at Borama in 1933 in which we focus on it later.

In 1952, Hussein Shaykh Ahmed (Kaddare) from, near Mogadishu invented yet another script known as Kaddare script. Kaddare Script has 41 letters. The direction of writing was from left to right. The technical commissions that evaluated scripts were in general agreement that the Kaddareh script was the most accurate indigenous script for the Somali language. For details of Kaddareh script see thesis about "written Somali" By Hussein Shaykh Ahmed, 1985.

QADI SOMALI SCRIPT.

Shaykh Abdirahman Shaykh Nuur was "born in 1906 at Qabribaxar a farming area in Awdal region at present day. When he was seven years of age his uncle Shaykh Barkhadle opened a Quranic School for young children at Shabelle, a small farming centre in the Western Somali. Shaykh Barkhadle called Sharif Ahmed Hassan to be the teacher of the School. Shaykh Abdirahman was one of the first children who enrolled in this school and was open minded within a short span of time he learned the first 15 chapters of the Quran also Shaykh Abdirahman learned thoroughly the Arabic phonology. After two years a dispute cropped up between Shaykh Barkhadle and the local community. As a response to his refusal to compromise with them a mosque and the Quranic school which are being erected by Shaykh Barkhadle were razed to the ground by the local community.

However, after this problem dispersed them, Shaykh Abdirahman arrived at Gabiley in the north west region of Somalia. There he learned the remaining 15 chapters of the Quran. An Arab clerk working with one of the richest persons in Gabiley helped him and taught him primary mathematics and business letter writing.

Shaykh Abdirahman's Father, Shaykh Nur was a well-known figure and he had a great knowledge in

Islamic law 'Shariah' due to his excellence and was nominated to be Qadi of Borama District. After Shaykh Abdirahman's father's nomination, Shaykh Abdirahman arrived in Borama and there he established the first Arabic School 'Madarasad' in the Protectorate. He was one of the pioneers of Education in Somalia. In 1933 Shaykh Abdirahman invented a unique independent Somali script to cut illiteracy amongst the Somali Society. A number of years Shaykh Abdirahman was a teacher of religion in the education department.

During those twenty years he had been in the education field and played a significant, important role in education. In addition to his vast knowledge of Arabic and religious studies he also attended several courses held for teachers from 1944-52 at Shaykh and passed the Departmental examinations. In 1952 he left the education field to join the judicial service to replace his father who died as Qadi in Borama District. Curriculum vitae is attached to this short history of Shaykh Abdirahman certified by the Director General, Ministry of Education in 1965 Saciid Abdirahman Ali (see page 14)

The Script.

Qadi Script has 21 consonants (hamza is excluded) and seven (7) vowels as I.M. Lewis mentioned. But Shaykh Abdirahman modified the vowels later on to 10 vowels. The script is written from left to right. Etymologically Qadi script is more developed than

Osmania.² The consonants are:-

b t j dh g x kh h d r s sh

c f q k l m n w y

The vowels which I.M. Lewis mentioned in his article are:-

a e i ii u uu oo

The modification of the Vowels are:-

a aa e ee i ii u uu o oo

Although Shaykh Abdirahman has no knowledge about Amharic language but by looking at Qadi Script it seems there is some affinity like its sister Osmania, especially the following symbols:-

b g x a c m n e u

Two texts written by Shaykh Abdirahman himself are published here with transliteration (in italics) and phonetically more accurate transcriptions (in Roman Type). Fairly literal English translations accompany the text (See Appendix 2).

---

2 The Gadabursi Somali Script I.M. Lewis 1958 London.

LATIN ALPHABET ADAPTATION ON SOMALI LANGUAGE

Missionaries were the forerunners of the Latin script orthography for the Somali. The last two decades in the 19th century Reverend Evangeliste De Larajasse and the Venerable Cyprien De Sampont wrote a practical grammar of the Somali Language.

In 1938 the British attempted to introduce a written Somali with the Latin script in one of their primary schools in Burco; this trial led to a demonstration in which three Somalis were killed. This attempt was serving the British interest only. The Wadaads saw the British action in much the same light as Maxamed Cabdulle Hassan saw the Roman Catholic efforts, and the plans were dropped.

In the South the Wadaads were less influential and the Latin script achieved moderate currency. By 1955 in a Mogadishu conference concerned with a Somali Script a permanent committee was formed and called itself 'Kulanka Afka Somaliyeed' (The Somali Language Meeting)[3].

The use of Latin Script for the Somali language was

---

[3] Somali experienced Language Politics and thought David D. Laitin 1977 Chicago.

developing in Europe rather than in Somalia. Foreigners and Somali Scholars contributed to the Latin adaptation of the Somali Language.

The consonant symbols are the same as in the system of Abdullahi Mahamud and BTUHO Panza, Lilias E. Armstrong, C.R.V. Bell, M.H.I. Galaal and B.W. Andrzejewski and M.M. Moreno and I.M. Lewis. Except for the differences set out in the table below[4]:

Abdullahi Mahamud and Bruno Panza	dh	sh	j	kh	hh	ʕ		y
Lilias E. Armstrong	ḍ	ʃ	j	x	ħ	ʕ	ʾ	y
C.R.V. Bell	ḍ	sh	j	kh	ħ	ʕ	ʾ	y
M.H.I. Galaal and B.W. Andrzejewski	ḍ	sh	j	kh	ħ	ʕ	ʾ	y, ÿ
I.M. Lewis	ḍ	sh	j	kh	ḥ	ʕ	ʾ	y
M.M. Moreno	ḍ	š	ğ	ḫ	ḥ	ʕ	ʾ	y
Shirreh Jama	dh	sh	j	kh	ch	c	ʾ	y

---

4 Somali Poetry An introduction B.W. Andrezejewski and I.M. Lewis London 1964.

Final steps towards Somali writing from 1960 until 1972.

In 1960 the ministry of education which was newly formed had set up a Somali Language Committee ordered to direct their steps towards evaluating the existing systems of writing. Their efforts were a useful introductory step and the nascent Somali Government was not strong enough to push their recommendations and to end the political dispute over the choice of script.

Conservative Muslim opinion in Somalia regarded the Latin script as a tool of Christianity and they said Latin Script is godless (*Laa diin*). The supporters of Far Somali (Osmania) viewed the Latin Script as a symbol not only for Christianity but of Colonialism and national humiliation. The Latin supporters on the other hand considered all invented scripts as costly and unfavourable to the era of technological progress and rejected the Arabic Script on the basis of its unsuitability for adaptation to the Somali phonology which is rich in vowels compared to Arabic.

By 1966 the technical commission that evaluated scripts was in general agreement that the Kaddare Script was the most accurate indigenous script for the Somali language, As we mentioned before. This UNESCO

Commission evaluated no less than ten unique Somali national scripts.

When the Somali Revolutionary Government came into power through military Coup led by Major General Mohamed Siyad Barre in 1969. They decided to increase their efforts towards the introduction of a national orthography. In order to practice this they recalled and enlarged the Somali language Committee and directed it to prepare school text books and adult literacy materials, but left the choice of script undecided.

On 21 Oct, 1972 the Supreme Revolutionary Council and the council of secretaries (Ministers) announced that they had decided on the Latin script. Vocally they declared Somali to be the Sole official language of the state. The occasion took place at the third anniversary of the Revolutionary government. During the celebration the president addressed his speech to the public mentioning the historical decision. Helicopters were continuously dropping leaflets in the capital Mogadishu showing the new alphabet and Slogans were fixed on the streets. All civil servants and army personnel were ordered to learn the new script within not more than three months. Soon Somali became the one and the only official language of all administration and public business. The foreign languages were being left for special purposes only.

The daily news-paper 'Xidigta Oktobar' played an important role for somali language study. New terms and new words were being used scientifically and literally. The news-paper was providing texts to help with quick learning for the Script.

Finally, the Somali National Theatre gave generous aid to the spreading of literacy. Songs and playwrights (Hees hawleed) were introduced describing its use and importance as a Somali official language.

CONCLUSION

The Somali language had no official and accepted orthography until 1972, several systems of writing were in private use and were more locked to certain areas, employing the Arabic or Latin character or Sometimes newly invented alphabets in the first half of the 19th century.

When the country became independent in 1960 it was urgently needed that the Somali language should become the official language in the new state. The Somali government set-up a special department in the ministry of education to put the final point on the chronic problem of Somali script writing.

However, none of the successive governments before the 1969 Revolution was able to conclude a national orthography, since the question of the choice of alphabet became a political and religious issue.

When the revolutionary government came into power in 1969 they put into their charter the introduction of a national orthography, they recalled and enlarged the Somali language commission and instructed them to prepare school books and adult literacy material, but left the choice of script undecided.

In October on the third anniversary of the Somali Revolutionary government, the Somali President

CONCLUSION

Mohammed Said Barre declared the supreme revolution council and the ministers had decided on the Latin script to be the official language of the State.

APPENDICES

APPENDIX 1
(Letter of Recognition)

MINISTRY OF EDUCATION   March 10, 1965

SHEIKH ABDURAHMAN SHEIKH NUR

The Director General ,
Ministry of Education ,
MOGADISCIO.

    Sheikh Abdurahman Nur is one of the oldest Sheikhs of Borama who helped to the maximum for the introduction of education in the country.

    He joined the Education Department in 1944 at the the express request of the Department and left in 1952 to join the judicial service to replace his father who died as Kadi in Borama Distric.

    During his service with the Education Department Sheikh Abdurahman Nur proved to be a man of high calibre ad dignity who commanded the respect of all . In addition to his vast knowledge of Arabic and religious studies , he also attended several courses held for teacher from 1944/52 at Sheikh and passed the Departmental Examinations.

(Sayeed Abdurahman Ali)
DIRECTOR, I DEPARTMENT

MINISTRY OF EDUCATION   March 10, 1965

Shaykh ABDURAHMAN Shaykh NUR
The Director General,
Ministry of Education,
MOGADISCIO.

    Shaykh Abdurahman Nur is one of the oldest Shaykhs of Borama who helped to the maximum for the introduction of education in the country.

He joined the Education Department in 1944 at the express request of the Department and left in 1952 to join the judicial service to replace his father who died as Kadi in Borama District.

During his service with the Education Department Shaykh Abdurahman Nur proved to be a man of high calibre and dignity who commanded the respect of all. In addition to his vast knowledge of Arabic and religious studies, he also attended several courses held for teachers from 1944/52 at Shaykh and passed the Departmental Examinations.

APPENDIX 2
(QADI SCRIPT)

I. M. LEWIS

TEXT II

A letter from Borama

[Qadi script text]

TRANSLITERATION AND TRANSCRIPTION

Bela'
Seyla'

Walal kii an je'la, Huseen. Salamad.
Walaal kii an je'laa, Huseen. Salaamad.
Anagu wa nabad. Rer zii wuhu yal Doobo.
Annagu waa nabad. Reer kii wuhu yaal Doobo.
Awr kii wewe wuha 'unay libah. 'Ali na wuu yimid.
Awr kii weyna wuha 'unaay libaah. 'Ali na wuu yimid.
Alebi yay na soo gaday. Noo soo dir sulug.

Alaabtii way na soo gaadhay. Noo soo dir subag.
Hooyma way timid. Walal ka Guuled wuhu
Hooyana way timid. Walaal kaa Guuleed wuhu
tagay Hargesa.
tegay Hargeysa.

Nuur Bile
Nuur Bile
Boorama
Boorama

TRANSLATION

Zeila.[1]

My beloved brother, Huseen. Peace.
I am well,[2] the *reer*[3] is at Dooho.[4]
The big burden camel has been eaten by a lion. 'Ali has come.
The goods have been received by us. Send us (some) ghee.
Our mother has come. Your[5] brother Guuleed has gone to Hargeisa.[6]

Nuur Bile,
Borama.[7]

[1] The ancient but now deserted town, at various times capital of the Muslim state of Adal (ninth/tenth-sixteenth centuries), on the north-west coast of the British Protectorate. Well-known place-names are here spelt as in common administrative usage in the Protectorate.

[2] Lit. 'it is peace', meaning above all spiritual equilibrium, not simply the absence of war. A rather perfunctory greeting, as here, the writer would be somewhat disturbed by the loss of the camel.

[3] Here, the nomadic hamlet, comprising a man's hut, sheep and goats, and possibly some milch camels and cattle, with his wife and children (by her) and probably a few families of close kin with their huts and stock. Each wife normally has one hut. The word *reer* is also used in other more general senses, as e.g. to mean 'people', but this is its basic meaning. For a general introduction to the structure of nomadic Somali society see my *The Somali lineage system and the total genealogy* (duplicated), Hargeisa, Somaliland Protectorate, 1957.

[4] A village in the west of the Protectorate.

[5] The article -*kaa* indicates that the person spoken of is more directly related to the recipient of the letter than to the sender. This possibly refers to the recipient and sender being of different mothers (Som. *kala hooyo*).

[6] The capital of the British Protectorate, of recent foundation and with no traditions of any considerable antiquity.

[7] The administrative centre of Borama District in the west of the Protectorate, home of Sh. 'Abdurahmaan author of our script.

Text V

Fragment of a Gabay by Ugaas Nuur

[Gadabuursi Somali script text]

Transliteration and Transcription

Gurayadu ilmala wahay digta mel arooriyahe
Gorayadu ilmaha wahay digtaa meel arooryahe
Shimbir tuna arooskay disto iyay ubad ka gesaye
Shimbirtuna arooskay disto ayay ubadka geysaaye
Iyakaba 'qala is dafiye awr ku kalaroone.
Iyakaba 'aqlays daafiyaye awr ku kala roone.

Translation [1]

The ostrich puts her child in the unsheltered plain.
But the bird [2] builds a large bridal house [3] to put her children in.
Their brains are not in keeping with the difference in their sizes.[4]

---

[1] This fragment comes from a well known *gabay* by *Ugaas Nuur*, see Text III, p. 149, n. 1.

[2] The Somali divide the feathered vertebrates into two main classes. Birds of prey are known collectively as *had-da*. Other (non-carnivorous) birds are called *shimbir-ta* usually translated in English as 'bird'. This is only partly correct as birds of prey are not *shimbir*. The ostrich belongs to neither class and is not considered as a bird. It is grouped with all game animals (*ugaad-da*) and is hunted, less frequently now than formerly, for its excellent fat used for making ghee. The antithesis is here between the great ostrich which shows less ingenuity in the care of its young than any small nesting bird.

[3] *Aroos-ka* is the house built for the bridal couple by the parents of the girl in return for the bride-price (*yarad ka*) paid by the husband and his kin. It also means bridegroom, or marriage. The *aroos* is in fact the newly constructed, abundantly equipped, especially adorned, house, built for the bride and her husband before the wedding and which they will probably occupy for the rest of their lives. In the interior it is the collapsible mat and skin-covered hut (*aqal*), built on a frame of boughs lashed together, of the nomads.

[4] *aqlays* from the Ar. *'aql* plus contracted is *Awr*, literally 'male burden camel', is used metaphorically here as a unit of large size. This is quite a common metaphorical use. These three lines have assumed almost the currency of a proverb to the effect that bulk and brawn are not the same as ingenuity.

APPENDIX 03:
A. INVENTED SOMALI SCRIPTS (CONSONANTS)

B. INVENTED SOMALI SCRIPT (VOWELS)

(INVENTED SOMALI ALKHPTA VOWELS)

INVENTED BY	SHORT VOWELS a e i o u	LONG VOWELS aa ee ii oo uu	YEAR OF INVENTION
Hussien Sh. Ahmed (Kadarre)	ⵊⵊ ⵌ ⵅ ⵂ ⵃ	ⵊⵊⵊⵊ ⵌⵌ ⵅⵅ ⵂⵂ ⵃⵃ	1952
Sh. Abdirajan Sh. Nuv	T H J ⴺ C	T HH ⵏ ⵌⵌ CC	1933
Osman Yusuf Keenadiid	ʃ l g h ɔ	ʕ ⵡ ⵎ ⵂⵎ	1920
Mahamed Ahmed Mohamud	c e 7 h m	c e 7 h m	1961
Mushaf Sh. Hassan	u d k g ⴺ	uu dd kk gg ⵌⵌ	1951
Ali Sh. Abdullahi Qudhi	ʒ ⴻ ⵙ ⵎ ⴸ	ʒʒ ⴻⴻ ʒ ⴾⴾ ⴸ	1952
Daud Mohamed T.	7 ʌ ʃ C U	- - - - -	1928
Hussien Mogni Waleq	b y ⵘ v L	- - - - -	1960
Mohamed Jama Salaad	π x h n z	π x h n z	1960
Kosain Kilowle	ʒ χ ⴲ ⵕ ⴱ	ʒʒ χχ ⴲ ⴲ ⴱⴱ	1960
Abdulkadir Adde M.	n c) ⵎ ⵌ	- - - - -	1961

S. Jidi Gayad -

APPENDIX 04:
THE REPORT OF THE SOMALI LANGUAGE COMMITTEE, 1961.

Mogadiscio,
15th May 1961.

THE REPORT
OF
THE SOMALI LANGUAGE COMMITTEE
1961

To

CONTENT:

COVERING LETTER FROM THE CHAIRMAN,

INTRODUCTORY REPORT,

TECHNICAL REPORT,

(x) APPENDIXES,

(x) ..... Appendix 1 shows the 18 scripts submitted for consideration, relatively;
Appendix 2, shown a proposed code system for the recommended script;
And appendix 3, : shows the organs of speech.

Mogadiscio,
15th May 1961.

THE REPORT
OF
THE SOMALI LANGUAGE COMMITTEE
1961

To
> His Excellency the Prime Minister,
> Dr. Abdulrashid Ali Sharmaarkeh.

Through:
> His Excellency The Minister
> of Education, Mr. Ali Garad Jama.

Your Excellency,

I have the honour to place before you this forwarding letter with the report of our Commission. Our work was the direct outcome of:

1. The Motion passed in the National Assembly on 16th September, 1960,
2. The consequent Motion passed in the Council of Ministers on 18th October, 1960.
3. The Minister of Education's letters of appointment of this Committee dated 8th December, 1960 and 1st January, 1961.

Under the above rulings a technical Committee of 9 Somalis was appointed at the end of October, 1960 to begin work on 1st November, 1960, conduct an advisory Commission on the urgent problem of written Somali, under the auspices of the Minister of Education. We were given the following instruction:-

> " You will investigate the
> best way of writing Somali,
> considering all the aspects
> of the language, with special
> eye on the technical side, and
> submit a report to the Government
> by March, 1961, showing
> the merits of all the script
> submitted to you for consideration;
> and if possible will recommend
> the best one for adoption
> in Somali."

The men appointed for this mission at the start were:

1. Musa H. Ismail Gelaal, — Chairman
2. Yassin Isman Yusuf, — Member
3. Mohamoud Saleh (Ladaneh), — Member
4. Dr. Ibrahim HaShi, — Member
5. Khalif Sudi, — Member
6. Mustaf Sheikh Hassan, — Member
7. Shirreh Jama, — Member
8. Hussein Sheikh Ahmed (Kaddareh), — Member
9. Yusuf Meigag Samater — Secretary

The appointment of these men was based on the following criterion:

1. Previous association of members with the problem of written Somali.
2. Knowledge of the structure of the Somali language and appreciation of its literature.
3. Distribution of the members among the various dialects of the language.
4. Consent of the various groups and associations supporting the scripts represented by the members appointed.

The fact whether all these members had family ties or came from the same department of the Civil Service was considered immaterial.

As soon as the work was started in November, the following serious administrative difficulties presented themselves to the committee:-

1. Yusuf Meigag who was appointed as the secretary of the committee could not be brought from Hargeisa owing to lack of funds.
2. Two very important members of the committee were transferred to outstations by their own Departments. These were:-
   (a) Mohamoud Saleh (Ledaneh), to Bosaso.
   (b) Kustaf Sh. Hassan of the Department of the General Affairs, to Ballad as D.C.
3. The generally retarding system of administration in Mogadiscio has caused an unnecessary delay in the work of the committee. On two occasions the

committee had to fall into recess of two or three weeks each time as a result of delays of correspondence, upon which progress of our work depended.

4. Appeals made to the Ministries under which those two men were serving asking for the return or the men to Mogadiscio received no result.

5. Khalif Sudi of the Ministry of works and communication could not attend meetings regularly enough as a result of pressure from his work. An attempt to release him for the sole service or the commission has also failed. As a result, (1) Mohamoud Jama, (2) Ali Sh. Abdillah, (3) Abukar Sh. Mohamed Fodaddeh, & (4) Addow Sh. Ali, were appointed as replacement, with your Excellency's kind consent.

6. Due to the fact that no financial provision for this was made scheme in the Council of Ministers' meeting in October last year, the committee's work could not run smoothly. Committee members who were offered some payment when they were appointed could not remain silent for 5 months without any pay. They had to raise their financial problem in every meeting. Answer given to them that it was not the practice for the Government here to give pay to people who conducted commissions of this kind and that they would be considered for remuneration at the end of their work would not satisfy them, specially when some of them had actually got pay in previous commissions they were in recently

7. The committee was affected by the generally acute housing problem of Mogadiscio nowadays, and we

could not find a proper office even in the first two months of our mission.

We staggered through all those and many other difficulties however, and thanks God, achieved some result.

Our committee was appointed as a technical committee with an advisory power. Our job was only to investigate this problem from the technical aspects, and then to propose an alphabet to the Government, which is technically acceptable. The political the religious and the social aspects of the problem have been left for the Government, the Parliament and the public to decide. If at all this committee had any other consideration in mind during its commission beside its technical investigation for a satisfactory orthography, it was the desire to recommend an alphabet which was, beside being technically acceptable was also both economical and progressive. We were conscious that:-

(a) We were a very poor nation which could not afford even 1£ million to buy a new printing facilities.

(b) We were living in an age of missile, when all developments and reforms should either be in the form of revolution e>r no reform at all.

Our judgement was based on those above criterion i.e. technicality, economy and progressiveness, and with those guiding principles in mind we recommended the sort at script which according to our sincere judgement possessed all these qualities. In addition this committee does not believe that by adopting an alphabet of one kind or another a country can change into a residence of infidels. A person could be Moslem using Chines Ideograph or be a Christian although using Arabic. What counts is the belief and manner of worship. This is the unanimous feeling of this Moslem committee. We could, acting under the influence of public emotion and the personal ambition of individual members of our committee, have adorned and recommended a hollow impractical orthography, and yet got both the morale and the material support of powerful groups of the public, etc. We preferred to follow our own consciences and recommended the most progressive script submitted for our consideration.

The bar critics of Mogadiscio have made acute criticisms, at first on the composition of the Committee and later on the quality of the members. They could not appreciate the inevitability of appointing into the same commission, people with such acture opposing views to discuss a topic of such national importance. It is true that the Committee consisted of men who for various reasons, acutely opposed one another on the choice of a national script, e.g. two were supporters of Osmania, two were supporters of Arabic, two Latin and two supported the other miscellaneous Somali orthographies. But who also should have been appointed, since these were the only people who had any academic knowledge of written Somali. It is the opinion of this Committee that although the task was hard and unpleasant the Government did the right thing when it put the problem into the hands of the very people who themselves created it by inventing all those conflicting scripts. If they succeeded well and good, but if they failed it was a sign that no one else might be able to do it.

Again, we feel that the reference of this problem to foreign experts of say the U.N.O. would only cause more suspicion and possibly ultimate failure. It was a Somali problem and Somalis alone should solve it.

Towards the end of our investigation two of our members have resigned on grounds of disagreement with the other members on points of choice between the scripts. They were, (1) Mr. Ibrahim Hashi, (2) Mr. Mohamoud Jama Afballad. This was rather unfortunate. However, it does not mean that we failed. It is only a matter of 2 men against 6. Actually, still 68% of us are united to complete the mission. Besides, small revolts like this are only understandable in discussing issues of this importance. The rumour that Kr. Yassin Isman had also resigned was unfounded. He asked for leave which was granted.

Finally, we beg to record here, a motion of gratitude to:-

1. The Minister of Education & his Assistant, tor their kind assistance for administering the commission.
2. The Director of the University of Mogadiscio, Mr. Michael Perone, and his Secretary Mr. Moh.

Mohamed Jama, for their kind assistance without which progress would have been difficult for us.

I am,

Sir,

Your Obedient Chairman,

M.H.I Galaal

Chairman
The Somali Language Committee

THE TECHNICAL REPORT

Part: 2

Before we show the technical analysis which lead us to our conclusion in this report we should like to give a concise account of the history of this problem of written Somali, Early in this centaury, several people Somalis and Europeans alike tried to introduce an alphabet for Somali. Among them were:

1. Our great National heroe, Sayid Mohamed Abdillah Hassan.
2. Mohamed Abdilleh Mayal of Barbera.
3. Isman Yusuf Kenadid.
4. Sheikh Abdulrahman Kadi of Borama. And
5. Captain J.S. King of Britain.

All these people tried the Arabic characters first, and all foiled in various stages, and for the some reason. The chief technical difficulty met by those early orthographers was the inadequacy of the Arabic vowel letters for writing Somali.

Arabic, owing to its structure, can be written with the omission of all the short vowels represented by the Harakas. In Somali if the harakas were omitted, the reader would have to guess the meaning from the context all the time, and this might not be possible in many cases.

To use the harakas throughout, on the other hand, would be impractical in every day use, as the Arabic Harakas would have to be supplemented at least by two additional new signs.

One of the orthographers, Mohamed Abdilleh Mayal went as far as producing primers using the Arabic characters, but the method was rejected by the people outright.

Sayid Mohamed Abdilleh Hassan too, abandoned the idea and depended on the memory or his disciples for the preservation of his literature, on grounds of difficulty to transcribe the 10 Somali Vowel sounds With the 6 Arabic vowel letters.

Isman Yusuf Kenadid tapped a completely different source. In 1920 he introduced an alphabet of his own, which, no matter what modern experts of orthographies may have to say against it, was certainly a great step forward in the exploration tor a satisfactory term or script for Somali. In this script the right number of vowel sounds of any Somali dialect were represented phonetically for the first time, and by comparing the two systems together, the Somalis realised fully why they always failed to use Arabic.

The technical quality of this script was the subject of a long chapter in this report but this Committee should here, like to record a unanimous vote of respect to Isman Yusuf for his initiative and zeal in the history of this problem of written Somali. It is not surprising that in subsequent years many more Somalis should have followed his footstep and evolved a cluster of over 20 scripts for their mm language, all based on the same principle and some of which might bo better than Isman's own device.

METHOD OF INVESTIGATION

As will be seen in the report our investigation wa devided into 5 different stops, 1, 2, 3, 4, & 5. In the first stage we confined our activities to the framing of a procedure to guide us in our work. This was an essential stop, specially, as our committee consisted of men who had never worked together before and who held sharply opposed views as to the best script to be recommended. For such a committee a clear sot of rules was necessary before any other step was taken into the technical study of the problem. As a result these rules were drafted:-

1. A register file to be opened for all the script presented for the language.
2. Any Somali wishing to submit a script to the committee for consideration should do so within 15 days from the day of announcement in the press.
3. The committee should consider only those scripts registered with the committee before the above

dote according to announcement.
4. Every member of the committee must maintain strict sense of impartiality in his consideration all the scripts presented as long as he is in the committee, and refrain from any kind of discrimination these scripts on grounds religion, geography, emotion, etc., but base his consideration only on the pure merits of each script.
5. No member should carryout any activity subversive to the good name of the committee or relationship between its members directly or indirectly.
6. The committee must make decision by means of majority vote, and by show of hand.
7. Half, of the committee members including the Chairman or the Vice Chairman or both can meet and make decisions.
8. A Chairman must be elected once a month.
9. Decisions concerning the scripts should be made after the merits of all scripts have been studied.
10. The Governing body of the committee should consist of Chairman, a Vice Chairman and two secretaries.
11. Information concerning the scripts under consideration must be secret and should be released to the public only under the kind consent of the Minister of Education, after discussion and agreement by the committee in session.
12. The following responsibilities will be left to the discretion of the chairman :-
    (a) Control of meetings,
    (b) Actions to be taken against a member on grounds

of ildiscipline.
13. As a preliminary step to ascertain the pure merit of each script presented for the language, the committee must do the following studies as a class:
   (a) The elementary phonetics of Somali
   (b) The elementary grammar of Somali
   (c) Making and study of charts and forms made to clarify the purr merit at each script, considering its deep potentialities as a modern script.
   etc.

14. Those above rules must be effective from the day they arc signed by the committee and approved by the Minister of Education.

The next step was to frame a second set of rules to be adopted as guiding principles in our search tor a satisfactory orthography tor Somali. This vas the most important step taken during the whole or our commission. The following 17 guiding. Principle were agreed upon by the committee in advance before any study was made on the scripts. These 17 principle show the ideal qualities our future orthography should have and we had to agree upon them at this stage. It was thought that it would be difficult tor the committee to agree upon such principles it the studies or the scripts were made first, a supporters of various scripts in the committee would have known, then, the weaknesses or the script they supported. We had no difficulty to approve them then, as no member knew whether the script he supported would fail or pass when related to these conditions. All members were present and participated in what was unanimou_s_ly agreed to be the basic requirements. These were the following principles:-

"Our future national orthography must, among other things, have the following qualities:

1. It must be phonetic.
2. It must be simple in setting.
3. It must not have any diacritics except those which were approved by the committee, i.e., one for accent and one to modify sounds.
4. It must not have any sign which have more than on e function.
5. It must not have assigns which are differentiated only by means of diacritics.
6. It must not have diacritics which are representing basic sounds or the language themselves.
7. It must have printing machines available in the country.
8. It must conform to the International Telegraphic Notations.
9. It must be standardised.
10. It must be based on alphabetic system.
11. It must be economical in all aspects.
12. It must have cursive as well as printing forms.
13. It must be susceptible to further modification without altering its basic foundation.
14. It must be applicable for all the Somali dialects.
15. It must be taught in schools.

16. It must be unique, i.e. it must not be composed of letters normally known to belong to others scripts.
17. It should not cause any confusion to its renders.

Our judgement of the scripts was to be based on those 17 factors. Items concerning religion and customs were at first included but were amended later on when the jurisdiction of our work was clearified This committee also felt that this problem con be tackled best by breaking it into steps and that this being the first, should be confined to the technical side of searching for a satisfactory alphabet only.

STEP 3.

In order to make every member of the committee more qualified for the mission which was by nature technical, lessons on the principle of orthographies, elementary phonetics and the basic structure of the Somali language and sounds, etc., were arranged within the committee.

The following are some of the notes prepared for the members as refreshers for them during the investigation:-

A CONCISE NOTE ON TELEGRAPH

Morse code is an acoustic telegraphy with two gongs of different notes. One note is called "dot" and the other, "dash" the dash being 3 times the duration of the dot. There are intervals between the letters and the longer intervals between words. Those dots and dashes are transmitted from wireless set with electromagnetic system despatched through the air by means of wire. They could also be despatched by means air waving a flag or by flashes of light.

Each gong has a basic sound equivalence recognized by all countries. Each language in the world, however has some sounds peculiar to it, for which special code signs have to be devised locally. In Somali for instance the sounds, (ع) ,(ظ) ,(ح) etc. which are peculiar to us are not represented in the international Morse, Code, and should therefore have special signs devised for them.

The following diagram shows the basic Latin alphabet and their value to the International Morse Code system:

A	.-	M	--	Z	--..
B	-...	N	-.	Ch	----
C	-.-.	O	---	1	.----
D	-..	P	.--.	2	..---
E	.	R	.-.	3	...--
F	..-.	S	...	4	....-
G	--.	T	-	5	.....
H	....	U	..-	6	-....
I	..	V	...-	7	--...
J	.---	W	.--	8	---..
K	-.-	X	-..-	9	----.
L	.-..	Y	-.--	0	-----

(A system proposed for Somali form within the

above is shown at the end of the report.)

PHONETICS

Phonetics is the branch of linguistic science that deals With spoken language and the investigation and analysis of the organs of speech used in producing the sounds and their sequences occurring in spoken utterances.

In its elementary stage, phonetic classifies the basic movements or articulations of the speech according to the state and direction of the air stream, and the degree of stricture o! the air passage. On this basic categories notions ore established which include plosives, <u>affricates</u>, nasals, laterals, rolls, fricatives, frictionless continuants and vowels.

Those are further subdevided according to the parts of the vocal apparatus involved in the articulation.

Active articulators are the lips, the tongue and the vocal cords, and passive articulators include the upper front teeth and the roof of the mouth. A part of the roof of the mouth called "soft palate", also functions as on active, articulator against the pharynx.

Consideration as to which active or passive articulators are involved lead to the establishment of another set of categories of articulations which include Bilabial, Labiodental, Dental, Alveolar, Palatal, Velar, Uvular, and Glottal. Any given consonant articulation may be broadly defined in terms of the two forgoing categories, by selecting an appropriate lable one from each category Vowels are classified according to the positions the tongue can occupy without constricting the air passage at any point so much as to produce friction in the articulation these positions are defined by stating which port of the tongue is raised, and how much.

A system of notation is essential for handling the above the best and the most widely known is the, "International Phonetic Alphabet, or I.P.A". This is based on the ordinary roman letters, supplemented by modified form of these and by letters imported from other alphabets, as well as some invented letter shapes, designed so as to harmonies as far as possible with the others.

There are also other modifiers in the form of accents and other diacritics. EACH SYMBOL IS ALLOTTED IN PRINCIPLE TWO A CERTAIN TYPE OF ARTICULATIONS, AND IT STANDS FOR IT EVER BY CONVENTION.

One of the fundamental requirements tor practical phonetic work is system at notation which is essential.

A CONCISE NOTE ON WRITING IN GENERAL

Writing is the graphic· counterpart or speech, and also, the most important method of record-keeping and of communicating ideas or sounds of the human voice by convenient marks or symbols, painted or drawn, traced or incised on paper, stone, mental or any other material, as a conventional device.

There are various kinds of writing, e.g. Logographic system in which each conventionalized character represents a in object with a word value. The Chinese system of writing is a good example of this.

There is also the syllabic system by which each sign represents a single syllable. The Japanese script is an example of this.

And finally there is the most highly developed form, the Alphabetical form, in which each symbol used has a single sound value.

HISTORY.

Before he learned to write men invented other ingenious way of doing this, by using everyday objects as tokens of symbols at what be wanted to say. For example, the Scythians, who inhabited southern Russia, once sent a letter to the Persians consisting of a bird, a mouse, a frog, and five arrows. It meant, "Persians, can you fly like a bird, hide yourselves in the ground like mouse, leap through swamps like e frog? If you cannot, then do not try to go to war with us: We shall overwhelm you with arrows."

Similar kinds of methods are found among various primitive peoples in other parts of the world.

The first real writing was primitive pictures drawn on animal bones, etc. It is not certain, however, to what extent those drawings were the beginning of art, or attempts to record events. In this kind at picture writing the written symbol represented an object or the idea behind an object, and had no connection with the spoken words as in late the phonetic writing was where the written symbol represented a sound of the voice.

About 3500 years ego, the alphabetic system which was much more convenient than the picture writings was developed, most probably from the SEMITES alphabet used some 3000 years ago. No one is certain how the semite alphabet itself came into being. It may have originated in Egyptian Hieroglyphics, or in another kind of picture writing such as that used in ancient Crete or in some other ancient Asian countries.

CONCLUSION.

An ideal writing system should be in agreement with the actual system of sounds, recognizing that some languages make distinction of sounds that pass, as it wore, unnoticed in other languages. A writing system to be easily learned and used must provide a clear means or distinguishing the phonemes of the language. The ideal thing is to have one sign for each phoneme. (To make the meaning of the word 'Phoneme', clear, let us take the Somali sign 'B'. Calling this 'A sound', we must realize that it has different pronunciation in the following three words, Bar - Hub - Laba. Nevertheless we use the same sign because the different pronunciations of this some sign do not indicate any contrast or meaning. Therefore it would be extravagance to use three different signs.

The evolution of many traditional orthographies date back to the time when the only important technique of graphic representation was handwriting. The number of separate character was not too important and they could be interlaced with each other in complicated ways. Modern machine writing including the typewrite and various typesetting machines for printing work best with simple writing system, using a limited number of characters which can be arranged in a single line. In addition, for the sake of ready recognition and ease of writing the use of 'Diacritics' should be avoided except to indicate accented syllables or tones.

In the case where the schools use a foreign language as the means of' instruction and communication and later on had to change to the mother tongue of the students, it is most advantageous to use same script for both languages. This means that the students do not have to learn to read and write a second time for the second language, but make a more or less direct transfer at their previously acquired abilities.

SUMMARY.

In considering the reduction at a language into a written form for the first time, the following criterion must be token as guidance:-

1. As far as possible, each symbol at the writing must stand for a single sound of the language all the time; in other word the writing must be 'Phonetic'.
2. When considering the devise or a script, the importance of its printing and commercial aspect must never be ignored.
3. The script Must be based on a pure alphabetic system and not on a backward form.
4. It there is a satisfactory world wide script or any other script with which the people are already acquainted, it is always more advantageous to adopt these than to plunge into a new script. This agrees with the principle, "A bird in the hand is worth then in the bush". Of course any part of an old script could easily be modified with less hazard than the invention or a new script.
5. 5. It the opinion or the people is deeply devided between two or more scripts, solution can be reached easily by moons of compromise.

It the above criterion are adopted then there is no reason for failure.

(An elaborate note all the structure or the Somali language and sounds is summarized in the report)

STEP No 4.

TECHNICAL ANALYSIS OF THE REPORT

As will be seen in the report 18 different forms of script have been submitted for consideration by various Somalis. Eleven of these, although their forms are based on the same principle were Somali scripts originated by Somalis themselves. Of the remaining seven four were various form of Arabic characters modified by Somalis for our language, and three were various forms of Latin characters also modified by Somalis for our language.

When these 18 scripts were received and the necessary administrative arrangements were made for the smooth running of the final investigation, two things were done about each script:

1. Every script was registered into a dia-graphic form.
2. Every script was studied thoroughly in a formal meeting of the Committee when
   (a) The script was written on a black board
   (b) Every member present, having copied it tor himself was given a short while to study it, (about 15 minutes).
   (c) Discussion was open on the script when every, member was allowed to give his free opinion about it and its merits recorded, good or bad.

STEP No 5.

Judgement was passed all the merits of each script by majority vote. (We did not record the minority view).

Part: 3.

INVESTIGATION

Committee Members.

1. Musa H. Ismail Gelaal,   Chairman
2. Shirreh Jama,   Vise Chairman
3. Hussein Sheikh Ahmed (Kaddareh),   Secretary
4. Ali Sheikh Abdillahi Qutbi,   Member
5. Dr. Ibrahim Hashi,   Member
6. Mohamed Jama (Afballad),   Member
7. Abukar Sheikh Mohamed (Fodaddeh), Member
8. Addow Sheikh Ali,   Member

FUNCTION.

"To investigate the best way of writing Somali and having considered all the aspects or the problem, submit a report to the Government by March, 1961, showing the merits of all the scripts presented for the language, and if possible to recommend one of them for adoption in Somali, paying special attention to the technical side of the problem".

As a prelude to a successful achievement of its aim, the Committee has first studied the basic structure of the language. As a result the following observations have been passed or record in a unanimous vote:-

1. The Somali Language

The Somali language is classed as a member of the Cushitic group or languages. Some or its member language are dead; i.e. not spoken in any country nowadays; e.g. the Ancient Egyptian languages. Others like the various dialects or the Gallas, are still flourishing.

It is an accepted fact that no language in the world is pure. Every language has some foreign words in it. This is due to the un-avoidable historical cultural and social contacts etc. which are going on all the time among the various peoples of the world. As a result we have a large number of foreign words in our language. The following is an estimated composition of our vocabulary:-

Words of Galla origin	75%
Words of Arabic origin	20%
Words of Indian origin	3%
Words of European origin	2%

The Somali language is considered to be rich in vocabulary and poetry etc. as any other language in the world. It is also believed that it has a difficult but well patterned phonetic, grammar and tonal rules.

The basic grounds of our language which should be represented in our future orthography are 34, excluding the numerals. 24 of these are consonantal sounds and

10 are vowels. The following categorical notes show the composition or our basic sounds, expressed in the International Phonetic Notations:-

Consonants.

Plosives: b, t, d, g, k, d(ظ)

Fricatives: h:(ح), X:(ح), S, q:(ق), ʃ:(ش), f, h, c:(ع)

Africates: tʃ:(ح) G : special sound in southern most dialects.

Nasals: n, m, ɲ : Special Rahanwein sound.

Laterals: L

Glottals: ʔ : (Alif hamza)

Rolled: r

Frictionless continuants: w, y.

Total consonantal sounds: 24.

Vowels.

Short: a i u e o

Long: aa ii uu ee oo

Total vowel sounds: 10

Total number of basic sounds in Somali: 34

As a result of its detailed studies in the language the Committee has also recorded the following observations and made following ruling as well.

1. The above 34 sounds are only to be represented in a "Broad Transcription". In a "Narrow Transcription" many more signs would be needed. Broad Transcription shows the basic sounds or primary articulations only, and ignores the detailed movements of the organs of speech in sound making (see Appendix No. 3). In a Narrow Transcription, however, one has to show the secondary articulations, etc. and therefore many more letters would be required.

2. Due to the fact that the Committee had to consider all the Somali dialects in its attempt to evolve a satisfactory alphabet for our language, two special sounds of the Upper Jubba dialects unknown to the other Somalis in the North as basic Phonemes had to be accepted. These are "ɲ", a palatal "n", and "ç" a rather strong palatal "y" with a small amount of implosion.

3. The Glottal stop, which is a rather uncommon vocal sound, should be represented in the form of a longish accent "/" just before the vocal sound marking it. This system was practiced by several of the devisors of the scripts submitted.

4. The Committee considered the inevitable need in our daily life of writing foreign words of names containing non-Somali sonnets, in our future orthography. A circumflex "^", used by one of the progressive devisors, Husein Sheikh Ahmed was

therefore considered and accepted. It will have the power of turning a Somali sound into its correlated foreign sound, e.g. "B" hearing this sign on top will be read as "P", "S" as "Z", "t" as "th" etc.

As a result of its detailed study of the basic sounds of the language, the Committee framed and passed the following signs as an ideal basis for their future investigations:-

CONSONANTS.

b t j ch kh c d r s sh d

g f q k l m n w h y

ny jy

WOVELS.

Short: a i u e o

Long: aa ii uu ee oo

Diacritics.

Accent, " ʕ " for glottal stop, (Alif Hamza)

Circumflex "^" Modifier of Somali sounds.

Total Sign: 35

Before launching the big job of investigating the merits of the 18 scripts submitted for consideration the Committee had to frame and pass a set of principles with which the value of each script may be detected.

This happened to be one of the most difficult jobs we came across during our commission, but we succeeded to overcame it. This contains the following seventeen main principles set as the standard factors for any scripts to fill in order to be considered as a potential script for our language in the future.

It was agreed that Among other things every script,

1. Must be phonetic
2. Must be simple in its lettering
3. Must not have many diacritics.
4. Must not have signs which have more than one function.
5. Must not have two or more signs differentiated by means of diacritics only.
6. Must not have diacritics representing basic sounds themselves.
7. Must have printing machines available in the country now.
8. Must conform to the International telegraphic notations.
9. Must be standardised.
10. Must be based on alphabetic system.
11. Must be economical in all aspects.
12. Must have a good cursive value.
13. Must be unique.
14. Must be applicable for all the Somali dialects.
15. Must be susceptible to modification.
16. Must be taught in schools.
17. Its letters must have consistent sound value.

The dangers guarded against by above 17 factors areexplained hereunder, categorically:

1. A modern orthography must be phonetic, ie, each letter in the alphabet must stand for a single sound unit permanently. This has the following advantages:
   (a) If an orthography is phonetic its number of letters will be small and as a result the cost of printing of its language will be much cheaper than it the script was not phonetic.
   (b) A phonetic alphabet is much easier to read and write. People learn to associate the characters with the sound once for all. There would not be any spelling mistake.
2. The letters of an alphabet must be simple in their settings, i.e. there must not be unnecessary, lines and looping in the letters. A character like this "𐒊" is impractical and therefore unacceptable.
3. Diacritics mean tiny sign over, under or through of the alphabet. They have the following technical disadvantages: .
   (a) All readers do not have the same good eye sight to see such tiny sign equally well.
   (b) People often forget to insert them and this omission causes a great deal or confusion and misrepresentations.
   (c) They increase the cost of the orthography.
4. Any sign which has more than one function in the orthography is very inconvenient. Take the letter (𐒆) in the Osmania orthography or the Arab (ي) these two signs have the quality of long pure vowels at

one time and consonantal quality at another. When they should be read as consonants or as vowels is governed by a complicated grammatical rule. In fact, as a result of the existence in the Arabic and the Osmania orthographies of serveral signs each having more than one function, it was not possible to use those two scripts for all the Somali dialects, without altering the face of the two scripts.

5. The (ح) and the (خ) in Arabic are differentiated by the tiny dot over the (خ). If this tiny dot is omitted by chance when one was using the Arabic alphabet for Somali one would cause the confusion of the two words,(لحٓ) and (لخٓ). The result would be (لحٓ) (لحٓ). Therefore diacritics are bad for modern use and must be avoided except on rare occasions when other methods fail.

6. (See above)

7. Handwriting is only of secondary importance in the use of orthographies. The most important need in the use of orthography is the printing. We need books, news papers, etc., printed cheaply. If an orthography for which printing machines are either unavailable or costly is adopted, then there will not be much chance for a successful national orthography.

8. One of the most important uses of orthography is in telegraphy An independent telegraphic communication is most necessary for a young independent country. An orthography which cannot be used in our telegraphic: communication, in

fact fails to fulfil half of our need and is: therefore useless. Either we must have an orthography which covers all our Governmental needs or use foreign language altogether.
9. Standardization of script is necessary for the sake of elegibility.
10. (See phonetic).
11. An ortography can be uneconomical in two ways:-
    (a) IF IT HAS A DELAYING EFFECT, THAN IT IS UNECONOMICAL.
    (b) If it is s difficult orthography like the Chinese or the Amharic, it will then be accessible only to the rich people. As a result literacy will be scarce and any thing that is scarce is expensive.
    (c) If the printing machinery is costly or unobtainable then the orthography will be uneconomical. The ideal orthography is therefore the one that is easy to learn, to print and HAS A QUICK RESULT.
12. An alphabet must have both cursive and printing forms for the sake or total practicality.
13. An alphabet must be unique in order to hove its own character. If it is composed of letters which are transposed from other orthographies it will not only lose prestige but may also cause confusion, especially if some of its letters belong to a foreign script already taught in the country, in which they have different sound value.
14. No language in the world is yet mastered by its people. New science, sounds and grammar, etc., are discovered continuously. For this reason no

orthography must be rigid. It must be possible to change its face without hazard to its basic foundation. It must be devised in such a way that any new sounds discovered may be represented in it without the addition of new signs to the script.
15. We hove only one language but our language contains several different dialects, and it would be uneconomical as well as illogical to have a different alphabet for each dialect. The cheapest thing is to have only one script which is so devised that the basic sounds of all the dialects may be represented with ease.
16. In Somali two orthographies are taught in Government Schools. These are Arabic and Latin. Several of the locally devised orthographies are also taught in private evening classes. The most convenient thing to do for us then, is to adopt some of those scripts which are already taught in our schools. It will be waste of time and money to adopt a type of alphabet unknown to our schools. The result will be, too many orthographies in our schools. (A bead-ache).
17. If we use Arabic script, for example, the value we give to each character must be same as the one it had when used for Arabic.

Having framed these seventeen principles to used as main factors with which the merits or each script could be detected the Committee started its analysis of the 18 scripts submitted to them.

THE SOMALI SCRIPTS, FORM 1 ('

1. Name or the script   Somali Script No.1
2. Name of its devisor   Husein Sheikh Ahmed (Kaddareh)
3. Year devised   1955
4. Number or letters it has   41
5. Direction it is written   From Left to Right
6. Number or forms it is written   Four, i.e. two cursive &. two printing.

ALPHABET.

Consonants:

    ᴆ Ω ȝ ᶓ ᴹ M Ʌ ᴆ Ш ᵹ H

    ᒥ Ƭ ᴴ ᵞ Ƶ ᴥ 8 ᵹ ɣ Ⅱ

Vowels (Short),   ᴌ ȝ ᴵ ᴧ ᵹ

Vowels (Long),   ᴌ̄ ȝ̄ ᴵ̄ ᴧ̄ ᵹ̄

(Printing Form)

Consonants:

    ᴄ ᴏ ᴢ ε ɪ ᴄ ᴆ ᴥ Ш ϵ ᴕ

    ᴄ ᴜ ɪ ᴇ ᴒ ᴂ ᴂ ᴕ ᴥ ϰ

Vowels (Short),   ᴦ ε ꝫ ᴧ ᴄ

Vowels (Long),   ᴦ̄ ε̄ ꝫ̄ ᴧ̄ ᴄ̄

As a result or their detailed study on this script the committee agreed to record the following facts in relation to the 17 principles passed at the detecting principles, as answers:-

FORM 1 (B).

1. Is it phonetic? — No
2. Is it simple in its lettering? — Yet
3. Have its letters any diacritics, if so how many have? — Yes-3
4. Has it any signs which have more than one function, if so how many? — No
5. Has it any letters which are difficult to distinguish, if so how many pairs? — No
6. Has it any diacritics used as letters themselves, if so how many? — No
7. Has it any printing machines available in the country, if so give
    (a) the approximate number of typewriters — No-NIL
    (b) the approximate number of printing machines — NIL
    (c) the approximate cost of its typewriter — No-NIL

8.	Could it be used in telegraphy immediately?	NO
9.	Is it based on alphabetic system?	YES
10.	Is it economical?	NO
11.	Has it a good cursive value?	YES
12.	Is it unique?	YES
13.	Could it be modified into amore acceptable form without changing its basic foundation?	YES
14.	Could it be applied for all the Somali dialects?	YES
15.	Is it taught in schools?	YES
16.	Is it standardised?	NO
17.	Is it used for another language, if so is it likely to cause any confusion?	NO

Advantages ... 9
Disadvantages ... 8

Therefore, it is considered as a satisfactory script and is submitted for further modification.

FORM 2 (A).

1.	Name of the script	SOMALI SCRIPT NO.2
2.	Name of its devisor	ABDULKADIR ADDE MUNYER
3.	Year devised	1961

APPENDICES

4. Number or letters it has   35
5. Direction it is written   From Left to Right
6. Number or forms it is written   ONE

ALPHABET.
(Cursive form)

Consonants:

Vowels,(Short),   THIS SCRIPT HAS
Vowels,(Long),   NO CURSIVE FORM.

(Printing Form)

Consonants: ᴄ ꜚ ᴊ ᴘ ꜗ ᴧ ᴌ ᴋ ꜙ ꜞ ᴜ
          ᴀ ᴄ ᴅ ᴆ ᴠ ᴌ ᴙ ᴜ

Vowels (Short), ᴎ ᴄ ᴧ ᴜ ᴊ

Vowels (Long),   NIL

Numerals: ᴊ ꜚ ᴄ ᴊ ᴛ ᴀ ᴙ ᴙ ᴏ

As a result of their study on this script the Committee agreed to record the following facts about it, as answers to these 17 guiding principles:

FORM 2 (B).

1. Is it phonetic?   No
2. Is it simple in its seting?   No
3. Have its letters any diacritics, if so how many have? No
4. Has it any signs which have more than one function, if so how many? No
5. Has it any letters which are difficult to distinguish, if so how many pairs? Yes 12 PAIRS
6. Has it any diacritics used as letters themselves, if so how many? No
7. Has it any printing machines available in the country, if so give
   (a) the approximate number of typewriters   No
   (b) the approximate number of printing machines   NIL
   (c) the approximate cost of its typewriter   NIL
1. Could it be used in telegraphy immediately?   NO
2. Is it based on alphabetic system?   YES
3. Is it economical?   NO
4. Has it a good cursive value?   NO
5. Is it unique?   NO

(It is based on the modern stenography)

6. Could it be modified into amore acceptable form without changing its basic foundation?   NO
7. Could it be applied for all the Somali dialects?   NO
8. Is it taught in schools?   NO
9. Is it standardised?   NO
10. Is it used for another language, if so is it likely to cause any confusion?   NO

Advantages ... 4
Disadvantages ... 13

As a result it is considered an unsatisfactory script.

FORM 3 (A).

1. Name of the script   SOMALI SCRIPT NO.3
2. Name of its devisor   SHEIKH ABDULRAHMAN KADI
3. Year devised   1930
4. Number or letters it has   28
5. Direction it is written   From Left to Right
6. Number or forms it is written   ONE

ALPHABET.

(Cursive form)

Consonants: (IT HAS NO CURSIVE FORM)

Vowels,(Short), -do-
Vowels,(Long), -do-

(Printing Form)

Consonants: ᶑ ᴣ ꝙ ʔ ʒ ⲧ ʃ Ȝ 6 ʓ
⟩ ⟨ F I ᴦ ʃ ч ɞ ꜱ ყ

Vowels,(Short), NIL ⊥ ᶜ ⏉ ᶝ
Vowels,(Long), ı ⊥ ᶜᶜ ⱨ ƽ

Numerals: (NO NUMERALS OF ITS OWN)

As a result of their study or this script, the Committee has agreed to record the following fact, about it, as answer to the 17 guiding principles passed:-

FORM 3 (B).

1. Is it phonetic? No
2. Is it simple in its seting? Yes
3. Have its letters any diacritics, if so how many have ? Yes, i.e. ⏉ and ᶜ
4. Has it any signs which have more than one function, if so how many? No
5. Has it any letters which are difficult to distinguish, if so how many pairs? Yes 5 PAIRS
6. Has it any diacritics used as letters themselves, if so how many? No

7. Has it any printing machines available in the country, if so give — No
   (a) the approximate number of typewriters — NIL
   (b) the approximate cost of its typewriter — NIL
   (c) the approximate number of printing machines — NIL
8. Could it be used in telegraphy immediately? — NO
9. Is it based on alphabetic system? — YES
10. Is it economical? — NO
11. Has it a good cursive value? — NO
12. Is it unique? — YES
13. Could it be modified into amore acceptable form without changing its basic foundation? — NO
14. Could it be applied for all the Somali dialects? — NO
15. Is it taught in schools? — NO
16. Is it standardised? — NO
17. Is it used for another language, if so is it likely to cause any confusion? — NO

Advantages ... 5
Disadvantages ... 12

As a result the script is considered to be unsatisfactory.

FORM 4 (A).

1. Name of the script   SOMALI SCRIPT NO. 4
2. Name of its devisor   ISMAN YUSUF KENADID
3. Year devised   1920
4. Number or letters it has   41
5. Direction it is written   Left to Right
6. Number or forms it is written   ONE

ALPHABET.

(Cursive form)

Consonants: ...

Vowels,(Short),   THIS SCRIPT HAS NO CURSIVE FORM.

Vowels,(Long),

(Printing Form)

Consonants: ⴘ ⴑ l M ⴙ O 7 ⴒ ⴓ ⴔ ⴘ
                 ⴙ ⴕ ⴖ ⴗ ⴘ ⴒ ⴙ ⴛ

Vowels (Short),   S 9 ⴙ Ꮝ ⴗ ⴜ ⴝ ⴞ ⴟ ⴠ

Numerals: S ⴡ ⴙ ⴛ ⴒ ⴢ ⴑ C U O

As a result or its detailed study on this script, the Committee has agreed to record the following fact, answering those 17 guiding principles:

FORM 4 (B).

1. Is it phonetic? — No
2. Is it simple in its setting? — Yes
3. Have its letters any diacritics, if so how many have? — No
4. Has it any signs which have more than one function, if so how many? — Yes 4, i.e. ሀ S ኁ ኁ
5. Has it any letters which are difficult to distinguish, if so how many pairs? — NO
6. Has it any diacritics used as letters themselves, if so how many? — NO
7. Has it any printing machines available in the country, if so give
    (a) the approximate number of typewriters available — YES-26
    (b) the approximate cost of its typewriter — Som. 900.00
    (c) the approximate number of printing machines available — NIL
8. Could it be used in telegraphy immediately? — NO
9. Is it based on alphabetic system? — YES
10. Is it economical? — NO
11. Has it a good cursive value? — NO
12. Is it unique? — NO.

13. Could it be modified into amore   NO
    acceptable form without changing
    its basic foundation?
14. Could it be applied for all the   NO
    Somali dialects?
15. Is it taught in schools?   YES
16. Is it standardised?   NO
17. Is it used for another language,
    if so is it likely to cause any
    confusion?   NO
         AT LEAST ELEVEN OF ITS LETTERS
    LOOK LIKE ONE OR OTHER OF LATIN LETTERS

Advantages   ... 7
Disadvantages ... 10

Disadvantages overweigh advantages, therefore it is considered unsatisfactory.

FORM 5 (A).

1. Name of the script   SOMALI SCRIPT NO.5
2. Name of its devisor
   Mustar Sheikh Hassan
3. Year devised   1951
4. Number or letters it has   42
5. Direction it is written   From Left to Right
6. Number or forms it is   ONE
   written

ALPHABET.

(Cursive form)

(THIS SCRIPT HAS NO CURSIVE FORM).

(Printing Form)

Consonants: ᠎ℓ ᡀ ℊ ℨ ⱨ ℛ ⅆ ο ⱪ
ᠯ ⱬ ⱨ ℊ ∩ ⱷ Ⴔ ᴜ ⱴ ℊ
ℎ ℳ ℊ

Vowels (Short) ⱴ ⱷ ⱨ ⱷ ⱬ
Vowels (Long) ⱴⱴ ⱷⱷ ⱨⱨ ⱷⱷ ⱬⱬ
Numerals: l ⱴ ⱨ ℰ ⱬ ℊ ⱴ ⱷ Ⴔ ο

As a result of their detailed studies on this script the Committee has agreed to record the following facts about it in answer to these 17 guiding principles framed to show the merits of the scripts.

FORM 5 (B).

1. Is it phonetic? — No
2. Is it simple in its setting? — YES
3. Have its letters any diacritics, if so how many have? — YES, 3, i.e. ᠯ ⱨ ⱨ
4. Has it any signs which have more than one function, if so how many? — Yes, 2, i.e. THE TWO SHORT VOWELS, ⱨ ℓ

5. Has it any letters which are difficult to distinguish, if so how many pairs? — NO
6. Has it any diacritics used as letters themselves, if so how many? — NO
7. Has it any printing machines available in the country, if so give
   (a) the approximate number of typewriters available — NO, NIL
   (b) the approximate cost of its typewriter — NO, NIL
   (c) the approximate number of printing machines available — NIL
8. Could it be used in telegraphy immediately? — NO
9. Is it based on alphabetic system? — NO
10. Is it economical? — NO
11. Has it a good cursive value? — YES
12. Is it unique? — YES. BUT HAS NO PRINTING FORM.
13. Could it be modified into amore acceptable form without changing its basic foundation? — YES
14. Could it be applied for all the Somali dialects? — NO
15. Is it taught in schools? — YES
16. Is it standardised? — NO

17. Is it used for another language, if so is it likely to cause any confusion?   NO, NOT USED FOR ANOTHER LANGUAGE IN THE COUNTRY.

Advantages   ... 7
Disadvantages ... 10

Disadvantages overweigh advantages, therefore it is considered unsatisfactory.

FORM 6 (A).

1. Name of the script   SOMALI SCRIPT NO. 6
2. Name of its devisor
   DAUD MOHAMED
3. Year devised   1928
4. Number or letters it has   25
5. Direction it is written   From Left to Right
6. Number or forms it is written   ONE

ALPHABET.

(Cursive form)

Consonants:

Vowels (Short)   IT HAS NO CURSIVE FORM

Vowels (Long)

(Printing Form)

Consonants: ՌՃՏՃՃՀՏ𝑁𝛾Ͻ

ɣ ⱥ ẞ ʋ ᵽ ſ ᴜ ᴧ ı ⱥ ӽ

Vowels (Short), ʇ ʔ ſ c ʋ

Vowels (Long), NIL

Numerals: (NO NUMERALS)

AS a result of their study on the script, the Committee has agreed to record the following facts about it in answer to these 17 guiding principles framed to above the merits of the scripts:

FORM 6 (B).

1. Is it phonetic? — NO
2. Is it simple in its setting? — YES
3. Have its letters any diacritics, if so how many have? — NO
4. Has it any signs which have more than one function, if so how many? — NO
5. Has it any letters which are difficult to distinguish, if so how many pairs? — NO
6. Has it any diacritics used as letters themselves, if so how many? — NO
7. Has it any printing machines available in the country, if so give
   (a) the approximate number of typewriters available — NO

    (b) the approximate cost of its typewriter   NIL

    (c) the approximate number of printing machines available   NIL

8. Could it be used in telegraphy immediately?   NO
9. Is it based on alphabetic system?   YES
10. Is it economical?   NO
11. Has it a good cursive value?   NO
12. Is it unique?   NO. IT IS BELIEVED TO BE CLOSELY ASSOCIATED WITH AMHARIC.
13. Could it be modified into amore acceptable form without changing its basic foundation?   YES
14. Could it be applied for all the Somali dialects?   NO
15. Is it taught in schools?   NO
16. Is it standardised?   NO
17. Is it used for another language, if so is it likely to cause any confusion?   NO

Advantages   ... 5
Disadvantages   ... 12

    Disadvantages overweigh advantages, therefore it is considered a bad script.

FORM 7 (A).

1. Name of the script   SOMALI SCRIPT NO.7
2. Name of its devisor   Ali Sh. Abdillahi Qutbi
3. Year devised   1952
4. Number or letters it has   41
5. Direction it is written   From Left to Right
6. Number or forms it is written   ONE

ALPHABET.

(Cursive form)

Consonants:

Vowels (Short):

Vowels (Long):

(Printing Form)

(This script has no printing form)

Numerals: (It use the same figure as the Latin script)

AS a result of their study on the script, the Committee has agreed to record the following facts about it in answer to these 17 guiding principles framed to above the merits of the scripts:-

FORM 7 (B).

1. Is it phonetic? NO
2. Is it simple in its setting? YES
3. Have its letters any diacritics, if so how many have? YES, 5 LETTERS.
4. Has it any signs which have more than one function, if so how many pairs? YES, eg,
5. Has it any letters which are difficult to distinguish, if so how many pairs? NO
6. Has it any diacritics used as letters themselves, if so how many? NO
7. Has it any printing machines available in the country, if so give
    (a) the approximate number of typewriters available NO
    (b) the approximate cost of its typewriter NO
    (c) the approximate number of printing machines available NIL
8. Could it be used in telegraphy immediately? NO
9. Is it based on alphabetic system? YES
10. Is it economical? NO
11. Has it a good cursive value? YES
12. Is it unique? NO. It has

85

many Latin letters in it, e.g., b,H,l,h,j,v,e,c, etc.

13. Could it be modified into a more acceptable form without changing its basic foundation?   NO
14. Could it be applied for all the Somali dialects?   NO
15. Is it taught in schools?   NO
16. Is it standardised?   NO
17. Is it used for another language, if so is it likely to cause any confusion?   NO

Advantages ... 5
Disadvantages ... 12

Disadvantages overweigh advantages; as a result it is classed as unsatisfactory script.

FORM 8 (A).

1. Name of the script — SOMALI SCRIPT NO. 8
2. Name of its devisor — Husein Hashi Halak
3. Year devised — 1960
4. Number or letters it has — 35
5. Direction it is written — From Left to Right
6. Number or forms it is written — ONE

ALPHABET.
(Cursive form)

Consonants:

Vowels (Short)

(Printing Form)

(This script has no printing form)

Numerals:

AS a result of their study on the script, the Committee has agreed to record the following facts about it in answer to these 17 guiding principles set for the detection of the merits of the scripts:-

FORM 8 (B).

1. Is it phonetic? NO
2. Is it simple in its setting? NO
3. Have its letters any diacritics, if so how many have? YES, 6, e.g., The 5 long vowels have discretion on top and one of the figures has a dash under neath.
4. Has it any signs which have more than one function, if so how many pairs? NO

5. Has it any letters which are difficult to distinguish, if so how many pairs? — NO
6. Has it any diacritics used as letters themselves, if so how many? — NO
7. Has it any printing machines available in the country, if so give
    (a) the approximate number of typewriters available — NIL
    (b) the approximate cost of its typewriter — NIL
    (c) the approximate number of printing machines available — NIL
8. Could it be used in telegraphy immediately? — NO
9. Is it based on alphabetic system? — YES
10. Is it economical? — NO
11. Has it a good cursive value? — NO
12. Is it unique? — NO. IT IS BELIEVED THAT HAS IT CLOSE ASSOCIATION WITH AMHARIC.
13. Could it be modified into amore acceptable form without changing its basic foundation? — NO
14. Could it be applied for all the Somali dialects? — NO
15. Is it taught in schools? — NO
16. Is it standardised? — NO

17. Is it used for another language,   NO
if so is it likely to cause any
confusion?

Advantages   ... 4
Disadvantages   ... 13

Disadvantages overweigh advantages. Therefore it is considered a bad script.

FORM 9 (A).

1. Name of the script   SOMALI SCRIPT NO. 9
2. Name of its devisor   MOHAMED JAMA SALAD
3. Year devised   1960
4. Number or letters it has   40
5. Direction it is written   From Left to Right
6. Number or forms it is written   ONE

ALPHABET.

(Cursive form)

Consonants:

Vowels (Short):

Vowels (Long):

(Printing Form)

(This script has no printing form)

Numerals: ٨ ٤ ٧ ۶ ϶ ȝ ع ⋀ ٩ .

AS a result of their study on the script, the Committee has agreed to record the following facts about it in on attached sheet, in answer to these 17 guiding principles passed to detect of the merits of the scripts:-

FORM 9 (B).

1. Is it phonetic? NO
2. Is it simple in its setting? YES
3. Have its letters any diacritics, if so how many have? YES, 6, e.g., ṅ ṅ ẓ ẋ ẋ ṯ
4. Has it any signs which have more than one function, if so how many pairs? YES, e.g.,
   THE 10 VOWELS ARE ONLY 5, AND THE VOWELS, "i" IS ALSO "y", AND THE "u" IS ALSO "w".
5. Has it any letters which are difficult to distinguish, if so how many pairs? YES, "..." "..."
   ALSO THE 10 VOWELS HAVE NO MEAN OF DIFFERENTIATION AT ALL.
6. Has it any diacritics used as letters themselves, if so how many? YES,
   FULL STOP MEANS ZERO AS WELL.
7. Has it any printing machines available in the country, if so give

(a) the approximate number of typewriters available — NO
(b) the approximate cost of its typewriter — NO
(c) the approximate number of printing machines available — NO
8. Could it be used in telegraphy immediately? — NO
9. Is it based on alphabetic system? — YES
10. Is it economical? — NO
11. Has it a good cursive value? — YES
12. Is it unique? — NO.
   IT HAS MANY LATIN LETTERS, E.G.,
   S M O E Y V X H J T N etc.
13. Could it be modified into a more acceptable form without changing its basic foundation? — NO
14. Could it be applied for all the Somali dialects? — NO
15. Is it taught in schools? — NO
16. Is it standardised? — NO
17. Is it used for another language, if so is it likely to cause any confusion? — NO

Advantages ... 3
Disadvantages ... 14

Disadvantages overweigh advantages; as a result this script is considered as an unsatisfactory.

FORM 10 (A).

1. Name of the script   SOMALI SCRIPT NO.10
2. Name of its devisor   KASSIM HILLOWLEH.
3. Year devised   1960
4. Number or letters it has   41
5. Direction it is written   From Left to Right
6. Number or forms it is written   ONE

ALPHABET.

(Cursive form)

Consonants:

Vowels (Short)

Vowels (Long)

(Printing Form)

(This script has no printing form)

AS a result of their study on the script, the Committee has agreed to record the following facts about it on the following sheet, in answer to these 17 guiding principles, set to show merits of the scripts:-

FORM 10 (B).

1. Is it phonetic?   NO
2. Is it simple in its setting?   NO
3. Have its letters any diacritics, if so how many have?   NIL
4. Has it any signs which have more than one function, if so how many pairs?   NO
5. Has it any letters which are difficult to distinguish, if so how many pairs?   YES, e.g., ꠋ ꠋ ꠋ ꠋ ꠋ ꠋ ꠋ ꠋ ꠋ ꠋ ꠋ ꠋ ꠋ ꠋ ꠋ ꠋ ꠋ ꠋ
6. Has it any diacritics used as letters themselves, if so how many?   NO
7. Has it any printing machines available in the country, if so give
   (a) the approximate number of typewriters available   NO
   (b) the approximate cost of its typewriter   NO
   (c) the approximate number of printing machines available   NIL
8. Could it be used in telegraphy immediately?   NO
9. Is it based on alphabetic system?   YES
10. Is it economical?   NO
11. Has it a good cursive value?   YES

12. Is it unique? NO. IT IS CLOSELY WITH THE LATIN.
13. Could it be modified into amore NO
    acceptable form without changing
    its basic foundation?
14. Could it be applied for all the NO
    Somali dialects?
15. Is it taught in schools? NO
16. Is it standardised? NO
17. Is it used for another language, NO
    if so is it likely to cause any
    confusion?

Advantages   ... 7
Disadvantages ... 10

Disadvantages overweigh advantages; therefore it is considered as an unsatisfactory.

FORM 11 (A).

1. Name of the script   SOMALI SCRIPT NO.11
2. Name of its devisor   MOHAMOOD AHMED MOHAMED.
3. Year devised   1961
4. Number or letters it has   41
5. Direction it is written   From Left to Right
6. Number or forms it is written   ONE

ALPHABET.

(Cursive form)

Consonants: [cursive consonant letters in two rows plus two more]

Vowels (Short) c ℓ ♂ ↷ ↷

Vowels (Long)   c ℓ ♂ ↷ ↷

(Printing Form)

(This script has no printing form)

Numerals: 1 ∠ ⊥ ϥ ⋎ 3 ♃ ∝ ♃ 10

AS a result of their study on the script, the Committee has agreed to record the following facts about it on the following facts shown, answering to these 17 guiding principles passed to show merits of the scripts:-

FORM 11 (B).

1. Is it phonetic?   NO
2. Is it simple in its setting?   YES
3. Have its letters any diacritics, if so how many have? YES, the 5 long vowels which have dash on top.

4. Has it any signs which have more than one function, if so how many pairs? NO

5. Has it any letters which are difficult to distinguish, if so how many pairs? YES, ɣ ɣ ɣ ɔ.

6. Has it any diacritics used as letters themselves, if so how many? NO

7. Has it any printing machines available in the country, if so give
   (a) the approximate number of typewriters available NIL
   (b) the approximate cost of its typewriter NIL
   (c) the approximate number of printing machines available NIL

8. Could it be used in telegraphy immediately? NO

9. Is it based on alphabetic system? YES

10. Is it economical? NO

11. Has it a good cursive value? YES

12. Is it unique? NO. IT IS CLOSELY WITH THE LATIN.

13. Could it be modified into a more acceptable form without changing its basic foundation? NO

14. Could it be applied for all the Somali dialects? NO
15. Is it taught in schools? NO
16. Is it standardised? NO
17. Is it used for another language, if so is it likely to cause any confusion? NO

Advantages ... 7
Disadvantages ... 10

Disadvantages overweigh advantages; therefore it is considered as an unsatisfactory.

FORM 12 (A).

1. Name of the script — ARABIC SCRIPT NO.1
2. Name of its devisor — MUSA H. ISMAIL GALAAL.
3. Year devised — 1952
4. Number or letters it has — 41
5. Direction it is written — From Right to Left
6. Number or forms it is written — 3, INITIAL, MEDIAL AND FINAL.

ALPHABET.

(Cursive form)

Consonants: ب ت ج ح خ د ذ ز س ش ذ
ع ح ف ق ک ل م ن ه ى

Vowels (Short) ۇ ھ ي 3 ى

Vowels (Long) ا ى و ٭ س

(Printing Form)

Consonants:

Vowels (Short) ITS PRINTING AND CURSIVE

Vowels (Long)   FORM ARE THE SAME

Numerals: ١ ٢ ٣ ٤ ٥ ٦ ٧ ٨ ٩ ٠

AS a result of their study on the script, the Committee has agreed to record the following facts about it as answer to the 17 guiding principles framed to show the merits of the scripts:-

FORM 12 (B).

1. Is it phonetic? — NO
2. Is it simple in its setting? — NO
3. Have its letters any diacritics, if so how many have? — YES, 10, ب ت غ ف ن ى ج خ ق ئ ؤ
4. Has it any signs which have more than one function, if so how many pairs? — YES, ى and و ARE BOTH VOWELS AND CONSONANTS.
5. Has it any letters which are difficult to distinguish, if so how many pairs? — YES, ب ت ج ح خ س ش ق ى

6. Has it any diacritics used as letters themselves, if so how many? NO
7. Has it any printing machines available in the country, if so give
    (a) the approximate number of typewriters available NO
    (b) the approximate cost of its typewriter NO
    (c) the approximate number of printing machines available NO
8. Could it be used in telegraphy immediately? NO
9. Is it based on alphabetic system? YES
10. Is it economical? NO
11. Has it a good cursive value? YES
12. Is it unique? YES
13. Could it be modified into amore acceptable form without changing its basic foundation? NO
14. Could it be applied for all the Somali dialects? NO
15. Is it taught in schools? NO
16. Is it standardised? NO
17. Is it used for another language, if so is it likely to cause any confusion? NO

Advantages   ... 5
Disadvantages ... 12

Its disadvantages overweigh its advantages. As result this script is considered as unsatisfactory.

FORM 13 (A).

1. Name of the script   ARABIC SCRIPT NO.2
2. Name of its devisor   SHEIKH AHMED ISMAN.
3. Year devised   1960
4. Number or letters it has   42
5. Direction it is written   From Right to Left
6. Number or forms it is written   3, INITIAL, MEDIAL AND FINAL.

ALPHABET.

(Cursive form)

Consonants: ب ت ج ح خ د ذ ز س ش ط
                ع ف ق ك ل م ن ه ى

Vowels (Short) ܁ ܂ ܃ ܄

Vowels (Long)   ا ى و و ى

(Printing Form)

Consonants:

Vowels (Short)   ITS PRINTING AND CURSIVE
Vowels (Long)   FORM ARE THE SAME
Numerals: ١ ٢ ٣ ٤ ٥ ٦ ٧ ٨ ٩ ٠

As a result of their study on the script, the Committee has agreed to record the following facts about it as answer to the 17 guiding principles framed to show the merits of the scripts:-

FORM 13 (B).

1. Is it phonetic? — NO
2. Is it simple in its setting? — NO
3. Have its letters any diacritics, if so how many have? — YES, 13, ب ت ج ح س ف ق و ى etc....
4. Has it any signs which have more than one function, if so how many pairs? — YES, THE ى THE و WHICH ARE BOTH VOWELS AND CONSONANTS.
5. Has it any letters which are difficult to distinguish, if so how many pairs? — YES, ب ت ج ح خ س ش ع غ ف ق etc....
6. Has it any diacritics used as letters themselves, if so how many? — YES, FULL-STOP MEANS ZERO
7. Has it any printing machines available in the country, if so give
   (a) the approximate number of typewriters available — YES, 200
   (b) the approximate cost of its typewriter — So.900/-

	(c) the approximate number of printing machines available	6
8.	Could it be used in telegraphy immediately?	NO
9.	Is it based on alphabetic system?	YES
10.	Is it economical?	NO. A HUGE SUPPLY OF PRINTING MACHINES WILL BE NEEDED
11.	Has it a good cursive value?	NO
12.	Is it unique?	YES
13.	Could it be modified into amore acceptable form without changing its basic foundation?	NO
14.	Could it be applied for all the Somali dialects?	NO
15.	Is it taught in schools?	YES
16.	Is it standardised?	YES
17.	Is it used for another language, if so is it likely to cause any confusion?	YES, IT IS CONFUSING

Advantages ... 6
Disadvantages ... 11

Its disadvantages overweigh its advantages. As a result, this script is considered as technically unsatisfactory.

FORM 14 (A).

1. Name of the script   ARABIC SCRIPT NO.3

APPENDICES

2. Name of its devisor   IBRAHIM HAS AND
                                FRIENDS.
3. Year devised   1960
4. Number or letters it has   41
5. Direction it is written   From Right to Left
6. Number or forms it is   3, i.e. INITIAL,
   written   MEDIAL AND FINAL.

ALPHABET.

(Cursive form)

Consonants: ب ت ج ح خ د ز س ش ط ظ
             ع غ ف ق ک ل م ن ه ی

Vowels (Short) وَ و ئ ی ا

Vowels (Long) وَ أو أی ی آ

(Printing Form)

Consonants:

Vowels (Short)   ITS PRINTING AND CURSIVE

Vowels (Long)   FORM ARE THE SAME

Numerals: ١ ٢ ٣ ٤ ٥ ٦ ٧ ٨ ٩ ٠

AS a result of their study on the script, the Committee has agreed to record the facts about shown hereafter answering the 17 guiding principles framed to show the merits of the scripts:-

FORM 14 (B).

1. Is it phonetic?   NO
2. Is it simple in its setting?   NO
3. Have its letters any diacritics, if so how many have?   YES, 15, ب ت ح خ غ ف ق و ى ....etc
4. Has it any signs which have more than one function, if so how many pairs?   YES, THE ى THE و WHICH ARE BOTH VOWELS AND CONSONANTS.
5. Has it any letters which are difficult to distinguish, if so how many pairs?   YES, (ب) (ت) (ح) (خ) (س) (ش) (ع) (غ) (ف) (ق)
6. Has it any diacritics used as letters themselves, if so how many?   YES, THE FULL-STOP IS ALSO ZERO
7. Has it any printing machines available in the country, if so give
   (a) the approximate number of typewriters available   YES, 200
   (b) the approximate cost of its typewriter   900/-
   (c) the approximate number of printing machines available   6
8. Could it be used in telegraphy immediately?   NO

9. Is it based on alphabetic system?   YES
10. Is it economical?   NO.
    A HUGE SUPPLY OF PRINTING MACHINES WILL BE NEEDED FROM OUTSIDE.
11. Has it a good cursive value?   YES
12. Is it unique?   YES
13. Could it be modified into a more acceptable form without changing its basic foundation?   NO
14. Could it be applied for all the Somali dialects?   NO
15. Is it taught in schools?   YES
16. Is it standardised?   YES
17. Is it used for another language, if so is it likely to cause any confusion?   YES,
    THE LONG ARABIC VOWELS WILL BE READ AS SHORT VOWELS

Advantages   ... 6
Disadvantages   ... 11

The disadvantages of this script overweigh its advantages. Therefore, it is considered as technically unsatisfactory for adoption in Somali.

FORM 15 (A).

1. Name of the script   ARABIC SCRIPT NO. 4
2. Name of its devisor   MOHAMED ABDI KHAIREH.

3. Year devised   1960
4. Number or letters it has   41
5. Direction it is written   From Right to Left
6. Number or forms it is   3, i.e. INITIAL,
   written   MEDIAL AND FINAL.

ALPHABET.

(Cursive form)

Consonants: ب ت ج ح د ر س ش ط
ع غ ڤ ق ل خ م ن ه ى

Vowels (Short) ا ئ ى ص و

Vowels (Long) آ أى ى ض وَ

ITS CURSIVE AND PRINTING FORM ARE THE SAME

Numerals: ١ ٢ ٣ ٤ ٥ ٦ ٧ ٨ ٩ ٠

AS a result of their study on the script, the Committee has agreed to record the following facts about it as answer to the 17 guiding principles framed to show the merits of the scripts:-

FORM 15 (B).

1. Is it phonetic?   NO
2. Is it simple in its setting?   NO
3. Have its letters any diacritics, if so   YES, 15,
   how many have ?   e.g. (_).

4. Has it any signs which have more than one function, if so how many pairs? — YES, e.g. THE (_) AND THE (_) WHICH ARE BOTH VOWELS AND CONSONANTS.

5. Has it any letters which are difficult to distinguish, if so how many pairs? — YES, "_" etc.

6. Has it any diacritics used as letters themselves, if so how many? — YES, ONE, THE FULL-STOP IS ALSO THE ZERO.

7. Has it any printing machines available in the country, if so give

   (a) the approximate number of typewriters available — YES, 200

   (b) the approximate cost of its typewriter — 900/-

   (c) the approximate number of printing machines available — 6

8. Could it be used in telegraphy immediately? — NO

9. Is it based on alphabetic system? — YES

10. Is it economical? — NO. A HUGE SUPPLY OF PRINTING MACHINES WILL BE NEEDED.

11. Has it a good cursive value?　　　YES
12. Is it unique?　　　YES
13. Could it be modified into a more　　　NO
    acceptable form without changing
    its basic foundation?
14. Could it be applied for all the　　　NO
    Somali dialects?
15. Is it taught in schools?　　　YES
16. Is it standardised?　　　YES
17. Is it used for another language,
    if so is it likely to cause any
    confusion?　　　YES,
    ARABIC CONSONANTAL SIGNS ARE USED AS
    VOWELS, AND ALSO AN ARABIC LONG VOWELS AS A
    SOMALI SHORT VOWELS

Advantages　　... 6
Disadvantages　... 11

The disadvantages of this script overweigh its advantages. Therefore, it is considered as an unsatisfactory script for use in Somali language.

FORM 16 (A).

1. Name of the script　　Latin SCRIPT NO.1
2. Name of its devisor　　SHIRREH JAMA.
3. Year devised　　1960
4. Number or letters it has　41
5. Direction it is written　From Left to Right

6. Number or forms it is written — 3, CURSIVE, PRINTING AND TELEGRAPHIC FORMS.

ALPHABET.

(Cursive form)

Consonants: *b A j ch x d r s sh*
dh z g f q k l m n w
h y ny jy

Vowels (Short): *a i u e o*

Vowels (Long): *á í ú é ó*

(Printing Form)

Consonants: b t j ch x d r s sh dh c
g f q k l m n w h y .

Vowels (Short): a i u e o

Vowels (Long): à ì ù è ò

Numerals: 1 2 3 4 5 6 7 8 9 0

AS a result of their study on the script, the Committee has agreed to record the following facts about it on the following form as answer to the 17 guiding principles framed to show the merits of the scripts:-

FORM 16 (B).

1. Is it phonetic?   NO

2. Is it simple in its setting? YES
3. Have its letters any diacritics, if so how many have? YES, 3, e.g. t, i, j.
4. Has it any signs which have more than one function, if so how many pairs? NO
5. Has it any letters which are difficult to distinguish, if so how many pairs? NO
6. Has it any diacritics used as letters themselves, if so how many? NO
7. Has it any printing machines available in the country, if so give
    (a) the approximate number of typewriters available — 5000
    (b) the approximate cost of its typewriter — 700/-
    (c) the approximate number of printing machines available — 12
8. Could it be used in telegraphy immediately? YES
9. Is it based on alphabetic system? YES
10. Is it economical? YES
11. Has it a good cursive value? YES
12. Is it unique? YES
13. Could it be modified into a more acceptable form without changing its basic foundation? YES

14. Could it be applied for all the Somali dialects?   YES
15. Is it taught in schools?   YES
16. Is it standardised?   YES
17. Is it used for another language, if so is it likely to cause any confusion?   YES, SOME OF THE CHARACTERS ARE GIVEN DIFFERENT VALUE.

Advantages ... 15
Disadvantages ... 2

Advantages overweigh disadvantages. As a result this script was considered as a satisfactory script.

FORM 17 (A).

1. Name of the script   Latin NO.2
2. Name of its devisor   ABDI KHAIREH AWALEH.
3. Year devised   1960
4. Number or letters it has   41
5. Direction it is written   From Left to Right
6. Number or forms it is written   3, CURSIVE, PRINTING AND TELEGRAPHIC FORMS.

ALPHABET.
(Cursive form)

Consonants: *b A g h q d r s*

     z x j c f v k l
     m n w p y

Vowels (Short)   *a i u e o*

Vowels (Long)   *aa ii uu ee oo*

     (Printing Form)

<u>Consonants</u>:   b t g h q d r s z x

      j c v k l m n w p y .

Vowels (Short)   a i u e o

Vowels (Long)   aa ii uu ee oo

Numerals: 1 2 3 4 5 6 7 8 9 0

AS a result of their study on the script, the Committee has agreed to record the following facts about it on the following form in answer to the 17 guiding principles, framed to show the merits of the scripts:-

FORM 17 (B).

1.	Is it phonetic?	NO
2.	Is it simple in its setting?	YES
3.	Have its letters any diacritics, if so how many have ?	YES, 3, e.g. t, i, j.
4.	Has it any signs which have more than one function, if so how many pairs?	NO

5. Has it any letters which are difficult to distinguish, if so how many pairs?   NO
6. Has it any diacritics used as letters themselves, if so how many?   NO
7. Has it any printing machines available in the country, if so give
   (a) the approximate number of typewriters available   5000
   (b) the approximate cost of its typewriter   700/-
   (c) the approximate number of printing machines available   12
8. Could it be used in telegraphy immediately?   YES
9. Is it based on alphabetic system?   YES
10. Is it economical?   YES
11. Has it a good cursive value?   YES
12. Is it unique?   YES
13. Could it be modified into a more acceptable form without changing its basic foundation?   YES
14. Could it be applied for all the Somali dialects?   YES
15. Is it taught in schools?   YES
16. Is it standardised?   YES
17. Is it used for another language, if so is it likely to cause any confusion?   YES,

SOME CHARACTERS ARE GIVEN DIFFERENT VALUE.

Advantages ... 14
Disadvantages ... 3

Advantages overweigh disadvantages. As a result this script was considered as a satisfactory script.

FORM 18 (A).

1. Name of the script — Latin NO.3
2. Name of its devisor — HALIMO MOHAMED ALI.
3. Year devised — 1960
4. Number or letters it has — 36
5. Direction it is written — From Left to Right
6. Number or forms it is written — 3, CURSIVE, PRINTING AND TELEGRAPHIC FORMS.

ALPHABET.

(Cursive form)

Consonants: *b A g y d r s j q f k c l m n v*

Vowels (Short): *a i u e o*

Vowels (Long): NIL

(Printing Form)

Consonants: b, c, d, f, g, h, l, m, n, r, s, t, y, j, k, q, v,

Vowels (Short)   a i u e o

Numerals: 1 2 3 4 5 6 7 8 9 0

AS a result of their study on the script, the Committee has agreed to record the following facts about it on answer to the 17 guiding principles framed to show the merits of the scripts:-

FORM 18 (B).

1. Is it phonetic? — NO
2. Is it simple in its setting? — YES
3. Have its letters any diacritics, if so how many have? — YES, 3, e.g. j, i, and t.
4. Has it any signs which have more than one function, if so how many pairs? — NO
5. Has it any letters which are difficult to distinguish, if so how many pairs? — NO
6. Has it any diacritics used as letters themselves, if so how many? — NO
7. Has it any printing machines available in the country, if so give
   (a) the approximate number of typewriters available — 5000
   (b) the approximate cost of its typewriter — 700/-

(c) the approximate number of printing machines available	12
8. Could it be used in telegraphy immediately?	YES
9. Is it based on alphabetic system?	YES
10. Is it economical?	YES
11. Has it a good cursive value?	YES
12. Is it unique?	YES
13. Could it be modified into a more acceptable form without changing its basic foundation?	YES
14. Could it be applied for all the Somali dialects?	NO
15. Is it taught in schools?	YES
16. Is it standardised?	YES
17. Is it used for another language, if so is it likely to cause any confusion?	YES, SOME CHARACTERS HAVE BEEN GIVEN DIFFERENT VALUE.

Advantages ... 13
Disadvantages ... 4

Advantages overweigh disadvantages. As a result this script was considered as a satisfactory script.

Having studied the merits of all the scripts presented for consideration the committee agrees to record the following facts about their general characteristics:-

1. All the Somali scripts are written in the same

direction as the Latin, i.e. from left to write, and none of them is written from right to left as Arabic, and this can mean a true gesture that Somalis prefer some characters based on the principle of the Latin script.
2. All the Somali scripts are based on the same system of letterings as the Latin.
3. Over a quarter of the total letters in the eleven Somali scripts are Latin characters.
4. All the eleven Somali scripts will be uneconomical.
5. Out or these eleven Somali scripts only two could be further modified into more acceptable forma without hazard to their basic foundation. Tbese are:-
    (a) The Somali script No, 1, devised by Husein Sh. Ahmed (Kaddareh)
    (b) The Somali script; No, 11, devised by Mohamoud Ahmed.
6. Eight of the eleven Somali scripts combine the following 3 major technical defects;.
    (a) Not being phonetic,
    (b) Uneconomical to the country,
    (c) Insusceptible for further modification.

These are:.
(a) The script No. 2, by Abdulkadir Addeh Munyeh,
(b) The script No. 3, by Sh. Abdulnhman Kadi,
(c) The script No. 4, by Isman Yusuf Kenadid,
(d) The script No. 5, by Mustaf Sh. Hassan,
(e) The script No. 6, by Daud Mohamed,
(f) The script No. 7, by Ali Sh. Abdillahi Qutbi,
(g) The script No. 8, by Husein Hashi Halek,

(h) The script No. 10, by Kassim Hillowleh.

As a result of the above technical defects combined by each of them the committee agrees to declare the above eight Somali scripts as unacceptable for use in our language as our future orthographies.

The Somali script No. 10,

(a) Has no printing form,
(b) Has a very difficult & confusing setting,
(c) Could not be further modified.

The Somali script No. 11,
(a) Has a difficult & a confusing setting,
(b) Has no printing form.

As a result they are considered unacceptable for adoption in Somali.

As a result of long discussions on the merits of the Somali script No. 1, the committee passed the following modification in it:-

1. The letter (ℰ) for the vary light (b) and the letter (ɫ) for the very light (d) are deleted as the two sounds they represent could be covered by the ordinary (b) and (d).
2. One or its written forms has been omitted.
3. The following letters have been altered-
   OLD FORM: (ð) (ƅ) (ɱ) (ʒ) (Σ) (м̇)
   NEW: (ɼ) (ɧ) (ɟ) (ɣ) (3) (м)
4. The system of numbering has been abandoned and the Latin system has been adopted.

5. The two diagraph, (𝒮𝓃) and (𝒥𝓃) are to represent the two upper Jubba special sounds, (ny) and (jy).

As a result of above modification following form of the Somali script No. 1. has been accepted to go into the semi final stage:-

FORM 19 (A).

1.	Name of the script	SOMALI SCRIPT NO.1
2.	Name of its devisor	FIRST DEVISED BY HUSEIN SH. AHME, (KADDAREH) & THEN MODIFIED BY THE COMMITTEE.
3.	Year devised	1952
4.	Number or letters it has	43 and 2 modifiers
5.	Direction it is written	From Left to Right
6.	Number or forms it is written	2, A PRINTING AND A HANDWRITING FORMS.

ALPHABET.

(Cursive form)

Consonants:

𝓑 𝒬 𝓏 𝓔 𝓟 𝓜 𝒜 𝒷 𝓜 𝒢 𝐻
𝒻 𝓛 𝓟 𝓎 𝓙 𝓶 𝒮 𝒻 𝓨 𝓤

Vowels (Short), 𝓊 𝒢 𝒾 𝓁 𝒢

Vowels (Long), 𝓊̄ 𝒢̄ 𝒾̄ 𝓁̄ 𝒢̄

(Printing Form)

Consonants:

ᄃ ᄆ ᄋ ᄌ ᄐ Ӏ ᄃ ᄒ ᄎ Ш ᄀ ᄇ
ᄃ ᄂ Ӏ ᄅ ᄂ ᄈ ᄇ ᄀ ᄈ ӿ

Vowels (Short), ᄂ ᄐ ᄏ ᄉ ᄃ

Vowels (Long), ᄂ̄ ᄐ̄ ᄏ̄ ᄉ̄ ᄃ̄

Numerals: 1 2 3 4 5 6 7 8 9 0

As a result of the above modification the Committee bas agreed to record the following facts about this script, in relation to the 17 guiding principles set to show the merits of the scripts:

FORM 19 (B).

1. Is it phonetic? — YES
2. Is it simple in its setting? — YES
3. Have its letters any diacritics, if so how many have? — YES, 3, ᅟᅮ H ᅟ.
4. Has it any signs which have more than one function, if so how many pairs? — YES ᅟ 8 ᅟ
5. Has it any letters which are difficult to distinguish, if so how many pairs? — NO
6. Has it any diacritics used as letters themselves, if so how many? — NO

7. Has it any printing machines available in the country, if so give
   - (a) the approximate number of typewriters available — NO
   - (b) the approximate cost of its typewriter — NO
   - (c) the approximate number of printing machines available — NO
8. Could it be used in telegraphy immediately? — YES
9. Is it based on alphabetic system? — NO
10. Is it economical? — YES
11. Has it a good cursive value? — YES
12. Is it unique? — YES
13. Could it be modified into amore acceptable form without changing its basic foundation? — YES
14. Could it be applied for all the Somali dialects? — NO
15. Is it taught in schools? — YES
16. Is it standardised? — NO
17. Is it used for another language, if so is it likely to cause any confusion? — NO. NOT USED FOR ANOTHER LANGUAGE.

Advantages ... 10
Disadvantages ... 7

Its advantages overweigh its disadvantages. Therefore it is considered satisfactory.

THE ARABIC SCRIPT.

The Arabic orthography as use for the Arabic language consists of the following 35 signs:-

ا ب ت ث ج ح خ
د ذ ر ز س ش ص
ض ط ظ ع غ ف ق
ك ل م ن و ه ي
َ   ِ   ُ   ْ   ّ   ٓ   ء

These 35 signs are divided into 3 different groups, each doing a special function in the language. The most important group is the consonants, numbering 28, i.e, from the "ا" to the "ي", which were devised to deal with the meaning of the word only; Cf, (نب) (خرج) (علم) (غعل).

The second group are the vowel points or the HARKAS, which are 4 in number. They are, َ ِ ُ ْ, and the letters, ا ي و, which, in addition to their consonantal value, are also the respective long vowels of the vowel points. Their function is to indicate the grammar only, e.g. (كَتَب) (كِتِب) (كُتُب) etc.

The last group are the Shadda, (ّ), the Madda, (ٓ) and the Alif hamza, (ء), which are special modifiers. The Shadda shows the doupling of consonants in the pronunciation and the Madda is used to show the melodic emphasis of the long vowels. The Alif hamza does two functions:-

1. It is used in place of the two vowel points i.e. the fatha and the kisra with the latter, "Alif", in the initial position; e.g., (أمانة) (إحسان).
2. It is fundamentally the sign for the glottal stop, eg, (مؤمنون) when it is often conducted by the (و).

The two functions of the long vowels ore governed by grammatical rule, i.e., next to vowel points they have consonantal value and next to consonants they themselves have the function of pure long vowels. This is the system which was later on adopted by Isman Yusuf Kenadid in the use of his two signs, (𐒆) and (𐒥), which correspond to the Arabic (ي) and (و).

This system of giving the (ي) and the (و) in Arabic and the (𐒆) and (𐒥) in Ismania double function has made both script very difficult for covering all the Somali dialects.

For example, in order to cover the Upper Jubbo dialects one has to accept the inclusion of two new special sounds or those dialects into the orthography, and the best way of representing these two sounds is by giving these four signs of the two respective scripts double functions. This is impossible here because the signs already had double function and they cannot bear a third.

What now remains is either to alter the shape or two of the other letters of the respective scripts or to invent new signs. Neither or these two ideas is acceptable either as there will either be a huge burden of new expenditure or confusion to the students of Arabic. In short neither Osmania nor Arabic ore acceptable because they fail to cover ell the Somali dialects.

A NOTE OF COMPARISON BETWEEN THE ARABIC & THE SOMALI LANGAUGES.

The Arabic language, as a member of the Semetic group of languages, has that special feature that the meaning of a word is contained in the consonants, usually 3 letters, and the vowels are only a grammatical function. As a result we see that the vowel signs are omitted in writing. Anyone who knows the Arabic grammar will have no difficulty to know whether the word, say, (ktb), in a context, means, kataba, kutiba or kutub. But to a men who does not know Arabic grammar, this is head-ache.

The fundamental structure of Somali is quite different. The vowels and the consonants are inseparable. If you want to write a word you have to show the vowel sounds as well as the consonants. Otherwise no one will be able to make bead or tail of what was meant; e.g., if you write the word, (س) "sar", omitting the vowel, the reader will not be able to know whether you meant, sar, sir or sur, in Arabic, (سَ) (سِ) (سُ), which are completely three different words. This means that if one has to use the Arabic script for Somali, one must, first of all, alter the Arabic vowel system completely, and one cannot do this either unless one is prepared to sacrifice one's own fluency in Arabic and at the same time incur heavy costs.

As a result of their observation on Arabic and their detailed studies on the merits of the 4 Arabic script, presented for consideration, the committee has agreed to record the following facts concerning the possible use of Arabic for Somali;-

1. Although Arabic generally has a good printing facilities, the number of machines available in the Somali Republic are tar inadequate for use in the Government machinery and in business, and to attempt to import sufficient supply will render unbearable cost and <u>delay</u>, making the adoption of Arabic totally uneconomical.
2. Excessive use of diacritics makes Arabic legibility generally doubtful.
3. Fundamentally Arabic has a very difficult setting. It contains 9 different croup or letters each differentiated only by tinny dots inserted over or under the letters.
4. Arabic has basically only 6 vowels while Somali has 10.
5. The attempt by some devisers to express the 10 Somali vowel sounds within the frame work of the 3 long Arabic vowels, the ا ي و, is just like putting a square peg in a round hole. Mr. Ibrahim Hoshi's form of Arabic script which is considered to be the best of its kind has the following rules in its vowels system:-

   LONG, (وُ) (ىُ) (و) (ى) (ا)

SHORT, (أُو) (أَى) (أَى) (آَ) (ئَ) (أَ)

The outcome was the following contusion:-

SOMALI WORD	ITS MEANING	ITS MEANING IN ARABIC
1. (سار)	to make incision	to become.
2. (طار)	clothes	to fly
3. (أولى)	to stay or refrain from	first
4. (قول)	a lizard	to stay
5. (سين)	mischief	the time when
6. (كون)	100.	to compose.

From those above examples we get the following information:-

1. The 3 Arabic letters, (ا) (ي) and (و), have long value when they are used as vowels. Here, when they were used for Somali they were given a short value, and the result is confusion. It is certainly unfair to expect a Somali youth who first becomes literate in Somali through thin system of Arabic script to remember to change the quality of several of the Arabic letters every time ho reads the Quran.
2. None of the Arabic scripts submitted could cover hole the Somali dialects.
3. None of the Arabic scripts could be further modified

into a more acceptable form without changing its basic foundation.

As a result the committee decides, most disappointedly, that the Arabic script should not be adopted for writing Somali.

THE LATIN SCRIPTS

In spite of their religious and other national emotions, the committee, having studied the set of Latin scripts submitted for consideration discovered that:-

1. They are all economical.
2. They could all be used for commercial purposes and for telegraphic communication immediately, i.e. one could use them in telegraphy straight away.
3. They could all accept further modifications without changes in their foundation.
4. They all have very simple letterings.
5. Their fundamental structure as shown in No. 5, of our guiding principles is less confusing then both the Somali as well as the Arabic groups of scripts.
6. Their general advantages overweigh their disadvantages.

As a result the committee agrees to submit them for further modification, and assort one more satisfactory single alphabet from them, to go into the semi final stage.

As a result of further study on the cluster of Latin scripts submitted for consideration the committee approves the following to modified form to go into the semi final stage:-

FORM 20 (A).

1. Name of the script   LATIN SCRIPT NO.1
2. Name of its devisor   SHIRREH JAMA.
3. Year devised   1961
4. Number or letters it has   45 sign include numerals.
5. Direction it is written   From Left to Right
6. Number or forms it is written   3, i.e. CURSIVE, PRINTING AND TELEGRAPHIC FORMS.

ALPHABET.

(Cursive form)

Consonants: *b t j ch kh d r s sh dh*
c g f q k l m n w
h y ny jy

Vowels (Short) *a i u e o*

Vowels (Long) *aa ii uu ee oo*

(Printing Form)

Consonants: b t j ch kh d r s sh dh
c g f q k l m n w h y ny jy / ^

Vowels (Short) a i u e o

Vowels (Long)   aa ii uu ee oo

Numerals: 1 2 3 4 5 6 7 8 9 0

The merits of this script are shown in the folowing form:-

FORM 20 (B).

1.	Is it phonetic?	YES
2.	Is it simple in its setting?	YES
3.	Have its letters any diacritics, if so how many have ?	YES, 3, i.e., i, j, t.
4.	Has it any signs which have more than one function, if so how many pairs?	NO
5.	Has it any letters which are difficult to distinguish, if so how many pairs?	NO
6.	Has it any diacritics used as letters themselves, if so how many?	NO
7.	Has it any printing machines available in the country, if so give	
	(a) the approximate number of typewriters available	YES, 5000
	(b) the approximate cost of its typewriter	700/-
	(c) the approximate number of printing machines available	12

8. Could it be used in telegraphy immediately?   YES
9. Is it based on alphabetic system?   YES
10. Is it economical?   YES
11. Has it a good cursive value?   YES
12. Is it unique?   YES
13. Could it be modified into amore acceptable form without changing its basic foundation?   YES
14. Could it be applied for all the Somali dialects?   YES
15. Is it taught in schools?   YES
16. Is it standardised?   YES
17. Is it used for another language, if so is it likely to cause any confusion?   YES.

IT IS USED FOR ANOTHER LANGUAGE IN WHICH THREE OF ITS SIGNS HAVE DIFFERENT VALUE.

Advantages   ... 15
Disadvantages   ... 2

Advantages overweigh disadvantages; As a result this script is considered as a satisfactory script.

FORM 21 (A).

1. Name of the script   (1) LATIN SCRIPT NO.1, (2) SOMALI SCRIPT NO.1
2. Name of its devisor   SHIRREH JAMA & HUSEIN SH. AHMED.

APPENDICES

3. Year devised — (1) LATIN SCRIPT: 1961, (2) SOMALI SCRIPT: 1952.
4. Number or letters it have — (1) LATIN SCRIPT: 45 sign, (2) SOMALI SCRIPT: 45 sign.
5. Direction it is written — Both from Left to Right
6. Number or forms it is written, — (1) LATIN SCRIPT: 3, (2) SOMALI SCRIPT: 2.

ALPHABET.

CONSONANTS:

(Cursive form)

Latin   *b t j ch kh d r x sh dh c g f q k l m n w h y*

Somali   (cursive Somali script letters)

VOWELS

(Short)   Long

Latin   *a i u e o*   *aa ii uu ee oo*

Somali   (cursive Somali script letters)

SPECIAL MODIFIERS

1. (/)   2. (^)

THE PRINTING FORMS OF THE TWO ALPHABETS RECOMMENDED

LTN, b,t,j,ch,kh,d,r,s,sh,dh,c,g,f,q,

k,l,m,n,w,h,y,a,i,u,e,o.

SOM, 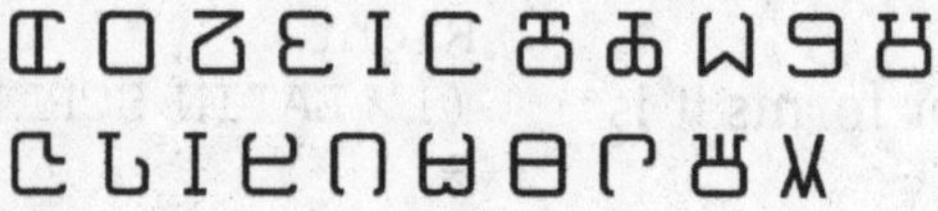

What ever our religious, nationalistic or even tribal sentiments might be in this problem of written Somali, there is no doubt that from the technical points of view, these two above scripts are by far the best of the 17 scripts submitted From the economical point of view, however, something can be said against Husein Sh. Ahmed's Somali script, but it is certainly better than all the other Somali scripts in most other aspects.

It will be seen in this report that preference was made to one script which had no printing machines against another which bad. For instance we recommended the Somali script No. 1, by Husein Sh. Ahmed Kaddareh which was not yet printed and rejected the Osmania and the Arabic scripts which had. The reason was that neither of the latter scripts:-

1. Could cover all the! Somali dialects as it was;
2. Was susceptible to further modification without hazard to its basic foundation.

CONCLUSION

According to the answers shown against the queries set in the 17 point guiding principles the most advantageous script has made itself crystal clear. It is the form of Latin script finalised in page 76. This script was submitted by Shirreh Jama and later on improved by the committee following favourable merits:-

1. It is economical.
2. It is phonetically accurate.
3. It is suitable for all our dialects.
4. It could be used for Telegraphic communication hence-forth.
5. It is very easy to road and write.

This script bas only one small technical disadvantage, and that is the contusion which might arise from the use of the letters (c) and the diagraph, (ch), which are used here to represent our (ع) and (ح), respectively. In English the sign (c), has two values. Some times it is read as (s), and some time as (k). The diagraph, (ch) also has two functions in English. Some times it as (k) and some times (j); Cf. (eat, ciycle, chest, technic). The, reason for using them for different sounds in Somali is pure economical. In tact their use in English and in Italia as well, the use of these signs is already confusing and additional value given to them in Somali will not make them any worst.

In short, it is the script that offers the best prospects to us, as a growing nation, and as a committee or men who, not only know about their langauge, but who understand the difference between their emotion and personal pride from their real needs, we recommended it for adoption as a matter first choice, and the Somali script devised by Husein Sh. Ahmed and modified by the committee as No 2 in the list. This committee could not recommended any other scripts.

The two script recommended are given in the following forms as script No 1, and No 2.

SCRIPT No 1 :
THE LATIN ALPHABET RECOMMENDED FOR ADOPTION IN SOMALI.

1. Name of the script   LATIN SCRIPT NO.1
2. Name of its devisor   SHIRREH JAMA.
3. Year devised   1961
4. Number or letters it has 43.
5. Direction it is written From Left to Right
6. Number or forms it is   3, i.e. Cursive,
   written   Printing and
                            Telegraphic forms.

ALPHABET.
(Cursive form)

Consonants: b A j ch kh d r s sh dh
             c g f q k l m n w
             h y ny jy

Vowels (Short) a i u e o
Vowels (Long) aa ii uu ee oo
 (Printing Form)

<u>Consonants:</u> b t j ch kh d r s sh dh
 c g f q k l m n w h y
 ny jy

Vowels (Short) a i u e o
Vowels (Long) aa ii uu ee oo
Numerals: 1 2 3 4 5 6 7 8 9 0
Special diacritics, (/) (^)

THE SCRIPT IN A CONTEXT OF SEVEN DIALECTAL PROVERBS

1. Ayach tag eel na reeb.
2. Intaad wach falin fiirso
3. La ma huraan waa cows jiilaal.
4. Haddaan fari jirin fahmo ma jirto
5. Ilko wada jir beey wach ku gooyaan.
6. Talo la diidaa tagoog jab beey leedahay.
7. Hashu laac-ca aragtay ee lun-ka hoose ma og tahay?

SCRIPT No 2. THE SOMALI SCRIPT RECOMMENDED FOR ADOPTION IN SOMALI.

1. Name of the script   SOMALI SCRIPT NO.1
2. Name of its devisor   HUSEIN SH. AHMED
                               (KADDAREH).
3. Year devised   1952
4. Number or letters it has   43.
5. Direction it is written   From Left to Right
6. Number or forms it is   2, i.e. Cursive
   written   and Printing Fs.

ALPHABET.

(Cursive form)

Consonants: ᛥ ᛩ ᛪ ᚠ ᛗ ᚨ ᛒ ᛖ ᚦ ᚺ ᚱ ᛚ ᛈ ᛃ ᛂ ᛘ ᛉ ᚾ ᚴ ᚢ

VOWELS

Vowels (Short) ᛚ ᚦ ᛁ ᚱ ᚳ

Vowels (Long) ᛚᛚ ᚦᚦ ᛁᛁ ᚱᚱ ᚳᚳ

(Printing Form)

Consonants: ⊓ ⊐ ⊃ Ɛ I ⊂ ƃ ƅ ⊔ ⊐ ⊔
C ᒪ Ɛ ⊓ ᖳ ⊟ Γ ⊎ ⊠

Vowels (Short), Ⴀ Ɛ Ɜ ⋀ C

Vowels (Long), ႠႠ ƐƐ ƷƷ ⋀⋀ CC

Special diacritics, (/) (^)

Numerals: 1 2 3 4 5 6 7 8 9 0

THE SCRIPT IN THE CONTEXT OF SEVEN DIALECTAL PROVERBS

1. *[handwritten script]*
2. *[handwritten script]*
3. *[handwritten script]*
4. *[handwritten script]*
5. *[handwritten script]*
6. *[handwritten script]*
7. *[handwritten script]*

ILAAHAYOW OQOON-NA HA NAGU CADAABIN RECHONA HA NOOGA TEGUN "AAMMIIN".

We are,

Sin,

Your Obedient Committee,

1. Musa H. Ismail Galaal,   Chairman,   _____
2. Shirreh Jama,   Vice Chairman,   _____
3. Husein Sh. Ahmed,   Art Secretary,   _____
4. Ali Sh. Abdillahi Qutbi, Art Secretary,   _____
5. Abukar Fodaddeh,   Member,   _____
6. Addow Sh. Ali,   Member,   _____

APPENDIX NO. 1

APPENDIX NO. 2

THE FOLLOWING CHART SHOWS A PROPOSED CODE SIGNS TO BE USED IN CONNECTION WITH THE RECOMMENDED ALPHABET IN TELEGRAPHY

CONSONANTS:

b	-...	c	-.-.
t	-	g	--.
j	.---	f	..-.
ch	-.-.	q	--.-
kh	-.-	k	-.-
d	-..	l	.-..
r	.-.	m	--
s	...	n	-.
sh	... .	w	.--
dh	-..	y	-.--

VOWELS

SHORT		LONG		
a	.-	aa	.-	.-
i	..	ii	..	..
u	..-	uu	..-	..-
e	.	ee	.	.
o	---	oo	---	---

NUMERALS

1	.----	6	-....
2	..---	7	--...
3	...--	8	---..
4	....-	9	----.
5	.....	0	-----

APPENDIX NO. 3

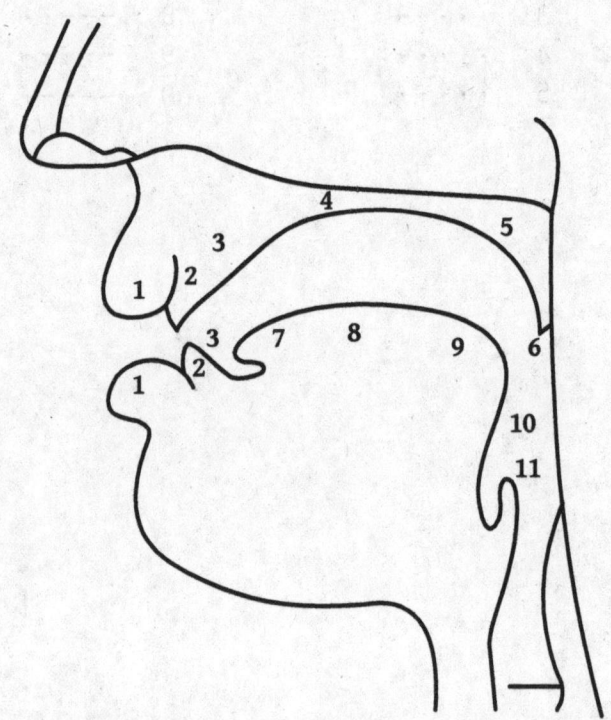

ORGANS OF SPEECH.

1. Lips.
2. Teeth.
3. Teeth-ridge.
4. Hard palate. (Velum).
5. Soft palate. (Velum).
6. Uvula.
7. Blade of tongue.
8. G. Front of tongue.
9. Back of tongue.
10. Pharynx.
11. Epiglottis.

BIBLIOGRAPHY

B.W Andrzejewski, The Development of Somali as a National Medium of Education and Literature. Journal African Languages 1979.

B.W Andrzejewski and I.M. Lewis Somali Poetry London 1964

Charles L. Geshkter Language Politics and University teaching In Somalia Journal of the Horn of Africa 1978.

David D. Laitin, Somali Experience, Language Politics and Thought, Chicago 1977.

Hussien Shaykh Ahmed (Kaddareh) Written Somali thesis for B.A. Degree 1985.

I.M. Lewis A Modern History of Somalia: Nation and State in the Horn of Africa London 1980.

I.M. Lewis The Gadabursi Somali Script Journal of African History London 1958.

Lewis, Herbert S. The Origin of the Galla and Somali Journal of African History, London 1966.

M. Noh Ali History of the Horn 1000 BC - 1500_AD aspects of Social and Economic change of the Rift valley to the Indian Ocean. Dissertation

Paper for PH.D. 1985.

Tom J. Farer War clouds on the horn of Africa, the Widening storm. New York, Washington.

Somalia and the World Proceedings of the International Symposium held in Mogadishu 1979.

www.ingramcontent.com/pod-product-compliance
Lightning Source LLC
Chambersburg PA
CBHW031545080526
44588CB00018B/2704